Hollywood Divided

HOLLYWOOD
DIVIDED

THE 1950
SCREEN DIRECTORS GUILD MEETING
AND THE IMPACT OF THE BLACKLIST

KEVIN BRIANTON

K UNIVERSITY PRESS OF KENTUCKY

Copyright © 2016 by The University Press of Kentucky

Scholarly publisher for the Commonwealth,
serving Bellarmine University, Berea College, Centre College of Kentucky, Eastern
Kentucky University, The Filson Historical Society, Georgetown College, Kentucky
Historical Society, Kentucky State University, Morehead State University, Murray State
University, Northern Kentucky University, Transylvania University, University of
Kentucky, University of Louisville, and Western Kentucky University.
All rights reserved.

Editorial and Sales Offices: The University Press of Kentucky
663 South Limestone Street, Lexington, Kentucky 40508-4008
www.kentuckypress.com

Cataloging-in-Publication data is available from the Library of Congress.

ISBN 978-0-8131-6892-0 (hardcover : alk. paper)
ISBN 978-0-8131-6894-4 (pdf)
ISBN 978-0-8131-6893-7 (epub)

This book is printed on acid-free paper meeting the requirements of the American
National Standard for Permanence in Paper for Printed Library Materials.

∞

Manufactured in the United States of America.

Member of the Association of
American University Presses

To John Salmond (1937–2013),
professor emeritus of history at La Trobe University

Contents

Photographs follow page 82

Abbreviations

DGA	Directors Guild of America
FBI	Federal Bureau of Investigation
HUAC	House Un-American Activities Committee
MPAPAI	Motion Picture Alliance for the Preservation of American Ideals
MPIC	Motion Picture Industry Council
RTDG	Radio and Television Directors Guild
SAG	Screen Actors Guild
SDG	Screen Directors Guild

Introduction

The Myth of the Screen Directors Guild Meeting

The *New York Times* Hollywood correspondent Thomas F. Brady wrote on October 22, 1950, that Soviet spies could not have developed a more fiendish plan to divide Hollywood than the loyalty oath drama that had torn apart the highly conservative Screen Directors Guild (SDG) over the previous few weeks. Brady believed that the impact of the proposed loyalty oath had split the Guild, the Motion Picture Industry Council, and the entire film industry. Hollywood directors may well have read that article on that Sunday morning and nodded agreement. That evening, every available film director would attend the Beverly Hills Hotel to witness a meeting that aimed to settle the divisive issue of loyalty oaths, blacklists, and the recall—forced dismissal—of the Guild president, Joseph L. Mankiewicz. It would prove to be a memorable and very late night.[1]

The SDG meeting of October 22, 1950, would eventually become a famous event in Hollywood history for all the wrong reasons. The meeting would touch on issues such as the House Un-American Activities Committee (HUAC) investigation into Hollywood, the blacklist of suspected Communists, patriotic loyalty oaths, and even anti-Semitism. It is legendary because the directors Cecil B. DeMille, John Ford, and Joseph Mankiewicz, along with many other celebrated figures, played prominent roles. Even small anecdotes from the meeting, such as Ford declaring, "My name is John Ford. I make westerns," have entered Hollywood folklore. The director and screenwriter Walter Reisch would eventually describe the SDG meeting as "the most tumultuous evening in the history of Hollywood." Its reputation has grown, and some historians have even argued the meeting was more about the American Constitution, free speech, and democracy than about the Hollywood blacklist and loyalty oaths.[2]

I

Each of the three principal directors had different paths to the meeting, and each would come to develop a distinct image as a result of it. Despite their political differences, the three men had a lot in common aside from being prominent film directors. All were determined men who demanded and won absolute control of their film sets. They were often figures of fear, respect, and loathing. DeMille in particular was notorious for his outbursts on the set, routinely humbling his loyal staff. His ferocity paid off: he ran a tightly disciplined crew that helped him cement his position, for more than four decades, as the most successful director in Hollywood history. More than that, he was a major celebrity in the media. His bald head and distinct features were as well known as his cinema, and his splendid speaking voice was recognized by millions across the United States through his national radio shows.

At the beginning of his cinematic career, DeMille was considered a relative failure compared with his brother, William, who forged a distinguished career in the theater. The brothers had been born to a theatrical family, and both had followed in the footsteps of their father, Henry, a playwright who worked closely with "the Bishop of Broadway," David Belasco. Cecil had worked in every aspect of theater from writing and acting to directing and lighting. He eventually tried his hand at cinema and codirected with Oscar Apfel *The Squaw Man* (1914), one of Hollywood's first feature films. An intensely driven man capable of long hours of work, he drew extensively on his background in Victorian theater to make a string of adaptations for the newly emerging art form of cinema. He rapidly built up a portfolio of successful films, and his efforts helped establish Paramount Studios, laying the groundwork for the Hollywood film industry. After initially sneering at the supposedly lesser art form, William would follow him out to Hollywood to begin his own directorial career.

A versatile director, Cecil B. DeMille often changed direction. In the late 1910s he became the master of domestic remarriage films, in which husbands and wives rediscovered each other after separation. He also directed a silent version of the opera *Carmen*, two biblical epics, and a historical epic about Joan of Arc. He was incredibly successful, becoming in the words of one of his harshest critics, Robert Sherwood, a "Hollywood Zeus." It was clear that he enjoyed making large-scale historical epics with a cast of thousands. However, the overruns on his big-budget films often brought him into conflict with studio heads. Indeed, in the late 1920s, after one budget blowout too many, DeMille's career collapsed and he was fired

2

from Paramount. He set up the DeMille Studio in response, but as driven as he was, he could not make it a success. For a short time it looked as though DeMille would disappear as Hollywood dealt with the dual threats of the arrival of sound and the Depression. He became a director for MGM, but his two-year contract was not renewed. In the 1930s he returned to Paramount on strict budgetary conditions, and he eventually reestablished his career with a popular series of historical epics and westerns. It is now no longer possible to separate the image of Cecil B. DeMille from his biblical epics, in particular *Samson and Delilah* (1949) and *The Ten Commandments* (1956), which dominated the latter part of his career. At the time of the SDG meeting, however, *Samson and Delilah* had only recently been released, and it represented just one biblical epic from the previous quarter of a century of filmmaking.[3]

Over the course of his career, DeMille became one of the driving forces of political conservatism in the film industry. He made many speeches attacking Communism and was particularly venomous about closed shops where only union members could work. DeMille had established the Cecil B. DeMille Foundation for Political Freedom to promote "right to work" laws. His campaign began when the American Federation of Radio Artists wrote to him on August 16, 1944. The federation wanted to impose a compulsory one-dollar levy on each of its members to pay for a campaign to keep closed shops. DeMille, who could clearly afford such a cost, refused to pay the levy. As a result the federation stripped him of his membership and he lost his position as a radio announcer. He campaigned against such measures from that point on. The foundation was a major part of DeMille's political life, and he took every opportunity to deliver speeches about the right-to-work issue for many years. Combined with his public stance against Communism, this campaign made DeMille one of the leading conservative figures in Hollywood. Even though he was close to seventy years old at the time of the meeting, he remained a strong personal, political, and cinematic force in the film industry.[4]

In his early days DeMille was famous for wearing an open shirt while working in the open air of silent-era sets. As he grew older and became a figure of the Hollywood establishment, he was more comfortable in impeccable three-piece suits. John Ford's dress style drifted in the other direction. In the 1930s Ford was often pictured as a dapper and serious-looking man in a formal suit. In his later years he was mostly photographed in rough working clothes. Ford was constantly chewing on handkerchiefs and often went through several a day. He had trouble with his eyes and would work with dark glasses and an eye patch to protect them. Like DeMille, Ford was genuinely feared on the set. In his younger days he had been a football player, and while not a particularly tall man, he could be intimidating to any actor. William de Mille had followed his brother Cecil out to Hollywood; John Ford had worked for his brother Francis, who was already established as a director in 1917. He would quickly move out of his brother's shadow and rise through the industry to become one of its pre-eminent filmmakers. His beginnings were as a stunt man, a cameraman, and even an extra riding in the Ku Klux Klan charge in D. W. Griffith's *The Birth of a Nation* (1915). It was when he became a studio director in the 1920s, however, that Ford's career and reputation began to grow, particularly after he directed the epic western *The Iron Horse* (1924). From that time he became one of the most respected and hardworking directors in the industry. He helped reestablish the American western in the sound era with *Stagecoach* (1939). By 1950 he had won Academy Awards for *The Informer* (1935), *The Grapes of Wrath* (1940), and *How Green Was My Valley* (1941).

Ford was firmly liberal in the 1930s, supporting Franklin D. Roosevelt in the presidential campaign of 1932. He was a key leader during the industrial disputes, believing that a financial crisis had been engineered by the banks, which controlled the film industry, in order to cut wages. Ford supported the Hollywood Anti-Nazi League, which united radicals and liberals in Hollywood against the rise of fascism, and he was once even quoted as saying, "If this be Communism, count me in." Ford was one of the directors who crowded into the living room of the director King Vidor on December 23, 1935, to contribute $100 to form the Screen Directors Guild. The Guild had so little clout early on that the producers would call meetings and not bother to show up. Yet it would grow in importance and strength over time. In 1939 the SDG reached an agreement with the studios to recognize the creative role of directors and their right to screen credits. After these initial fights, the SDG became an effective and successful labor organization for its members, establishing such policies as minimum wage standards and better working conditions for assistant directors. The SDG soon represented 95 percent of directors and assistant directors in Hollywood. In the eyes of the Federal Bureau of Investigation (FBI), Ford was part of a group within the SDG who had professed a "progressive position maintaining that a motion picture should carry a social or political message."[5]

When the Second World War broke out, Ford enlisted and directed wartime documentaries, two of which received Academy Awards: *The Battle of Midway* (1942) and *December 7th* (1943). After the war, his interest in westerns was revived, and he directed *My Darling Clementine* (1946), *Fort Apache* (1948), *3 Godfathers* (1948), *She Wore a Yellow Ribbon* (1949), and *Wagon Master* (1950). At the time of the climactic Guild meeting, he was completing *Rio Grande* (1950). Ford's politics had become more conservative during this period, and he joined the key Hollywood anti-Communist organization, the Motion Picture Alliance for the Preservation of American Ideals, in 1944. Despite his growing conservatism, Ford was always involved in the Guild at some level.

Joseph Mankiewicz was not a Hollywood pioneer like Ford or DeMille, but he had been active in Hollywood since the late 1920s, working his way up the career ladder. He had written title cards for silent films and had begun writing screenplays in 1929. Mankiewicz was just as feared on the set as Ford and DeMille, particularly by his assistant directors. In an industry where each level of the hierarchy struck fear into those below, colleagues thought Mankiewicz was not afraid of anyone. Like Ford, he had a brother, a prominent scenarist named Herman, who had worked in the film industry before him. Joseph was often dubbed "Mankiewicz Minor." Joseph once said that they would put on his tombstone: "Here lies Herm—I mean, Joe Mankiewicz." Herman was seen as one of the most brilliant writers ever to work in Hollywood. He collaborated with Orson Welles on the screenplay of *Citizen Kane* (1941), and many consider the older Mankiewicz brother to have been the driving force behind that landmark film. Both brothers were blessed with a tremendous sense of humor and enormous writing talent. Joseph was a popular man, but he had few close friends, and even these described him as elusive.[6]

Joseph Mankiewicz had something of a liberal reputation as a founding member of the Screen Writers Guild, and his screenplays reflected this political bias. One of his stories became the basis of the film *Diplomaniacs* (1933), which poked fun at the political intrigue of the period—depicting armaments manufacturers as the enemy of peace. He wrote dialogue for King Vidor's *Our Daily Bread* (1934), a "back to the land" fantasy of the Depression that advocated collectivist communes. As early as 1949, in his film *A Letter to Three Wives*, there was even a veiled reference to HUAC. He could not overtly criticize the committee, but in one scene, ostensibly an argument between a husband and wife regarding their future, the political tensions in America can be seen. The husband asks his wife if he could be reported as "un-American" for arguing his political case against a conservative client. Mankiewicz had also cowritten and directed a strong plea for racial tolerance in *No Way Out* (1950), which in the 1950s made a strong progressive stand. The film was released in August 1950, just before the SDG meeting. At the same time, his most famous film, *All About Eve,* also released in 1950, projected no overt political message.

Mankiewicz's other political activities cut across the idea that he was a liberal Democrat. He was considered to be on the political right and broke with other Screen Writers Guild members to campaign against the socialist candidate Upton Sinclair. Mankiewicz was reportedly against Sinclair because of his policy of raising taxes. Sinclair campaigned on an "End Poverty in California" platform, which called for taxes on super profits for film studios. MGM head Louis B. Mayer opposed Sinclair with an extensive radio campaign, and the studios applied a fair amount of pressure on their writers to work on the campaign. Mankiewicz wrote radio scripts on behalf of the "stop Sinclair" ticket. He also supported the Republican candidate Wendell Willkie in 1940.[7]

By 1950 Mankiewicz was no longer a minor player in Hollywood. Indeed, his output during the years around the meeting has rarely been rivaled, let alone surpassed. For *A Letter to Three Wives*, Mankiewicz picked up Academy Awards for best director and best screenplay. The SDG had already honored him for outstanding directorial achievement for the same film, and he would win the Guild's highest accolade again in 1951 for *All About Eve,* which would go on to win Academy Awards for best picture, best director, and best screenplay. In the same year he was also nominated for story and screenplay for *No Way Out.* By the time of the Guild meeting in October 1950, he was at the top of his game.

It was the anti-Communist whirlwind following the Second World War that brought this trio of Hollywood's top directors into open conflict at the Guild meeting in 1950. The meeting has been frequently quoted and referenced in books, documentaries, and most accounts of the blacklist period. Yet it has been so misrepresented and distorted that its history can only be called a myth. The myth goes something like this . . .

At the height of the blacklist era, with its witch hunts and paranoia about Communism, the film industry was in turmoil. HUAC was laying waste to those on the political left in Hollywood. A blacklist was under way, and this meant people would be denied work if even suspected of harboring Communist sympathies.

The SDG board of directors was bitterly divided on the issue of loyalty oaths—a legal statement declaring that a person was not a member of the Communist Party and did not support its ideology. On one side was the arch-conservative industry titan Cecil B. DeMille, a seasoned anti-union campaigner. He was one of the most formidable political figures in Hollywood and a rigid anti-Communist ideologue. DeMille had steadily gained complete control of the Guild over many long years and installed likeminded right-wing elders onto the board. His "DeMille Foundation for Americanism" was compiling information on liberal and progressive directors and actors that would ultimately be handed over to HUAC. DeMille wanted even more. Using his foundation, led by the infamous anti-union leader Tom Girdler, he wanted to crush political opposition from any source, seeing little or no difference between Communism and liberalism. The loyalty oath was the first step in a campaign to purge the Guild of Communists as well as any leftist liberals. This technique would then be repeated by unions across Hollywood and would spread across the United States. Those who resisted and did not sign would be put on a blacklist and be unable to find work again in Hollywood or anywhere else. The United States would have a nationwide blacklist.

Joseph Mankiewicz, the newly installed SDG president with little political experience, had been appointed by DeMille as a puppet. Although a Republican, Mankiewicz was edging toward liberalism. DeMille had seriously underestimated the caliber of his appointee. Mankiewicz had rejected the idea of a loyalty oath with the support of more-senior figures such as John Ford and George Stevens. This group had initially blocked the oath. DeMille was forced to wait until Mankiewicz was in France to strike back. His handpicked conservative allies George Marshall and Al Rogell pushed through the loyalty oath and aimed to lock it in with an open and signed ballot, which would mean the conservative Guild leadership would know who had voted for the measure and who had not. Such information would soon be transferred to the producers, and jobs would be lost. In the midst of the Red Scare, the ballot was supported by the vast majority of the membership: 547 to 14. The fear was real, as the Hollywood Ten had been imprisoned for contempt of Congress. Countless others were on other black- and graylists. In this atmosphere of political fear and danger, the membership turned to Mankiewicz to protest against the loyalty oath.

Mankiewicz had little effective influence, as the Guild's real power lay with its self-perpetuating fifteen-member board. Even though he was outgunned by the conservatives and was a political novice, Mankiewicz took the fight to DeMille, at one point throwing down the gauntlet by saying he would not sign the oath. DeMille was furious. Joining forces with powerful Hollywood gossip columnists such as Hedda Hopper and Louella Parsons, he orchestrated a smear campaign to begin to drive Mankiewicz from office. After letting loose the smear of Communism, DeMille and other conservatives then worked to complete Mankiewicz's removal. Working through the following day and night, DeMille directed SDG staff to print and distribute the ballots to dismiss Mankiewicz—which provided no opportunity to vote no. To avoid tipping off Mankiewicz, DeMille personally scratched out fifty-five names of possible opponents. The ballots were released, with motorcycle riders delivering the recall motion to every director in Hollywood. It would need the support of two-thirds of the membership, and Mankiewicz would be gone. He would then be placed on a blacklist and his career would be shattered.

Despite DeMille's attempts at secrecy, Mankiewicz's colleagues let him know about the recall. In response, Mankiewicz gathered his supporters, took out a legal injunction to stop the recall, and tried to call a general meeting to thrash out the issue. It was the only chance they had. They needed twenty-five directors to sign a petition to call such a meeting and rallied a younger generation of directors who were not as conservative. Searching throughout Hollywood, they barely met the quota to call a simple meeting. DeMille was not done yet—the SDG offices had shut their doors on a normal workday to preclude any such countermoves. Eventually, Mankiewicz found out when the offices were open, and the petition was registered. The meeting would go ahead.

DeMille and his forces then realized they had a fight on their hands and released a long explanation in a telegram to all members. Mankiewicz and his supporters started to hit the phones to rally support for the beleaguered president. They found that their supporters were fearful. DeMille arrived at the meeting on October 22, 1950, armed with detailed dossiers on his political opponents. DeMille's political ally Rogell was searching for Elia Kazan in order to further discredit the directors supporting Mankiewicz. Fortunately, Kazan had already fled in fear of DeMille using his past to destroy Mankiewicz.

As the meeting progressed, the SDG descended into a form of civil war. The stakes could not have been higher. Mankiewicz began the meeting with a clear account of the events leading to the recall. DeMille was invited to respond. In his obsession with showing the foreign influences at work, he read off a list of suspect Communist groups with which the twenty-five signatories were affiliated, arguing that if Mankiewicz remained as president, these Communist forces would win. He went further and began to read each name, pronouncing the names of the foreign-born directors with an eastern European or Yiddish accent: "Veely Vilder" for Billy Wilder, "Fred Tzinnemann" for Fred Zinnemann. It had a distinct anti-Semitic tinge. All hell broke loose, and DeMille was booed from all parts of the membership.

Both Fritz Lang and Rouben Mamoulian chastised DeMille for his racism, as they both felt apprehensive about speaking with an accent. Those who had served their country during the Second World War were incensed by his actions. George Stevens told DeMille that he was "freezing his arse off" at the Battle of the Bulge while DeMille was counting his capital gains in Hollywood. George Stevens then resigned from the board, demanding that DeMille just go. Frank Capra had resigned earlier. Don Hartman summed up many of the feelings of the directors when he demanded that DeMille resign for his grotesque actions during the meeting. Still DeMille would not budge, and he looked certain to triumph. He remained standing after the onslaught and had retained control of the board. All seemed lost. Then John Ford rose to his feet and began praising DeMille and his cinema. The liberals thought their case had collapsed. Mankiewicz was despondent. Ford was such a revered figure in the Guild—indeed, was one of its founders—and he was the only one whom DeMille genuinely feared. Ford paused; you could have heard a pin drop. Then Ford told DeMille that he did not like him or a damn thing he was doing. He called for the resignation of the board, which was quickly adopted. Using his immense personal authority, he brought DeMille crashing down. The SDG meeting was over. The loyalty oath was destroyed. DeMille and his cohorts were left in the dust.

It is a great story, and some of it is even true.

I

The House Un-American Activities Committee Arrives in Hollywood

Cecil B. DeMille, John Ford, and Joseph L. Mankiewicz all worked in a highly charged and divisive political environment. Some form of political surveillance had been going on in the fledgling film industry since the First World War. Even in the early stages of his career, DeMille had been involved in political intrigue. He was head of the Hollywood chapter of the citizens group the American Protective League, and in this role he worked with army intelligence to observe and report on people suspected of being pro-German. The American Protective League had the task of checking the "loyalty, integrity and character" of some directors hired to make sensitive wartime productions. For example, DeMille signed off on the integrity of the director Victor Fleming when he was considered for the role of director making documentaries. When the Russian revolution took place in November 1917, known or suspected Communists began to be closely watched. DeMille's role would continue after the war. According to his brother, William, Cecil vouched for his patriotism to federal agents after he had planned to hear the Communist William Z. Foster speak at Charlie Chaplin's house in 1922.[1]

Progressive political activity would reach a high-water mark in Hollywood in the 1930s, when people became alarmed at the growth of fascism in Europe. The threat led to the development of a united front between liberals and radicals in groups such as the Hollywood Anti-Nazi League. At the same time, the film industry was also a bastion of political conservatism, which looked on the growth of the league with horror.

While surveillance of Communists had begun during the First World War, it reached a more intense level during the Second World War. The release of *Mission to Moscow* in 1943, with its pro-Stalin message applauding a wartime ally, led the FBI director, J. Edgar Hoover, to believe that Communists were now prevalent throughout the film industry. A report to Hoover said that the Communist leadership had "thrown caution to the wind" in its efforts to gain control and its previously hidden leadership was visible as a result. He reacted by beginning a comprehensive and system-atic surveillance of the film industry, ranging from scrutiny of industrial issues and the political activities of directors, actors, and writers to the content of films. At one point in 1944 Hoover demanded a report by the fifteenth of each month on the infiltration of Hollywood by Communist agents and ideas. This grew into a file of several thousand pages called "Communist Infiltration—Motion Picture Industry (COMPIC)," tracking the activity of known and suspected Communists.[2]

The FBI believed the Screen Directors Guild to be one of the key sources of power in Hollywood. An earlier report, from 1943, said that if the Communists controlled the SDG, it could lead to "the production of motion pictures sympathetic to the cause of Communism and the political economy of the Soviet Union." Among those listed by the FBI as possible Communist sympathizers in the SDG were former president George Stevens, because of his work on Russian relief drives, and Orson Welles, the director of *Citizen Kane,* for his backing of the maritime union leader Harry Bridges. Michael Curtiz was accused of following the Communist line and of being inexperienced and often handing over the direction of *Mission to Moscow* to the technical director and suspected Communist Jay Leyda. The actor and director Irving Pichel was seen as "active in circles allied to the Communist Party." The German émigré Fritz Lang was either "a Communist" or a follower of the "Communist Party line." However, even the FBI did not believe that the entire SDG membership was Communist, or even that a majority was so inclined.[3]

The wartime alliance with the Soviet Union stopped federal conserva-tives and the FBI making open efforts to highlight Communist activity during the war, but the same constraints did not affect state investigations. As early as 1941 the Tenney Committee—calling itself the Fact Finding Committee on Un-American Activities in California—concluded that Hollywood was a "veritable mecca for the Communist cultural clique." State senator Jack Tenney wrote the reports, which saw Hollywood as a central focus for Communists in their efforts to take over the country. Originally a Democrat in 1936, Tenney was elected as a Republican in 1942 and served until 1954. He had switched political platforms when he was defeated for reelection to Local 47 for the American Federation of Musicians, blaming his defeat on Communists. He began investigating Communist involvement in Hollywood in 1941, alleging that from 1934 the Soviet Union had paid large sums of money to capture key trade unions within Hollywood. Produced almost every year since 1941, and running to thousands of pages, these reports detailed anti-Communist activity and listed alleged Communist front organizations throughout California. Despite describing itself as "fact finding," the Tenney Committee did not provide strong evidence for its claims. It would label a group as a Communist front on the slightest of evidence, leading one journalist to quip, "A Communist is any, who disagrees with Tenney." Many of those appearing before HUAC in 1947 had some form of contact with Tenney during the war years.[4]

While the Tenney Committee was writing its reports, the conservatives in Hollywood coalesced to form the Motion Picture Alliance for the Preservation of American Ideals (MPAPAI) on February 5, 1944, to combat the specter of Communism. This was partly a response to the industrial turmoil within the film industry. Tensions would explode in the wave of industrial action in 1945–1946, a series of massive postwar labor strikes spanning numerous industries. It proved to be the largest strike action in American labor history, focusing on shortages and inflation but also discipline, company policies, and firings. The industrial environment in Hollywood was particularly poor, with violent clashes on picket lines. Many people in the film industry, including the actor and Screen Actors Guild (SAG) board member Ronald Reagan, thought the disputes were Communist-inspired. Members of the MPAPAI included some of the most celebrated figures in Hollywood. The directors John Ford, Leo McCarey, and Sam Wood joined the producers Cecil B. DeMille and Walt Disney, along with the union leader Roy Brewer of the conservative International Alliance of Theatrical Stage Employees to establish the group. Its members would form the bulk of the "friendly witnesses" at the HUAC hearings in 1947.[5]

With Cold War tensions increasing, the Republicans, using strong anti-Communist rhetoric, made clear gains in the 1946 elections, picking up many seats in the House of Representatives. The rise of the conservatives ended the Democrat control that had dominated American politics throughout the Roosevelt and Truman administrations. Republican power in the House of Representatives and Senate led to a series of congressional investigations, the most prominent of which was the HUAC inquiry into Communist involvement in the film industry. The committee began its investigation by interviewing selected labor and industry leaders in the film industry in March 1947 in closed-door hearings. Listening to anti-Communist figures in Hollywood did not provide the HUAC chair, J. Parnell Thomas, and the investigator Robert Stripling with enough evidence to proceed with a full investigation. They needed the FBI, which had been building up a massive dossier of Communist involvement in Hollywood over the previous three years. At first Hoover did not want HUAC linked to the FBI, but Thomas and Stripling promised discretion when they contacted Los Angeles FBI agent Richard B. Hood for support. Hoover then arranged to assist the committee on the basis that the FBI remain unidentified, and he eventually testified to it in an open session on March 26, 1947, where he declared that "the aims and responsibilities" of HUAC and the FBI were the same: "the protection of the internal security of the Nation." Hoover used the opportunity to argue that the Communist Party was penetrating many "public opinion mediums," particularly the film industry, and that it would achieve its goal of capturing American institutions through infiltration of unions and creative outlets. Hoover said, "I would have no fears if more Americans possessed the zeal, the fervor, the persistence and the industry to learn about this menace of Red fascism. I do fear for the liberal and progressive who has been hoodwinked and duped into joining hands with the Communists." Hoover's testimony to HUAC was a blurring of the lines between liberals and radicals. Congress ordered that 250,000 copies of Hoover's address be printed and distributed. The FBI and HUAC were now allies. It would be a rocky relationship, but essentially the FBI would gather the evidence, and the committee would disclose it.[6]

The full HUAC investigations began in October 1947. Nineteen subpoenas were issued, and SDG members Herbert Biberman, Edward Dmytryk, Lewis Milestone, Irving Pichel, and Robert Rossen were among those called to testify—an odd selection as Milestone and Pichel were not Communists. The mixture of Hollywood glamour and the sinister threat of Communism proved irresistible for the media: the hearings drew so much attention that spectators needed to wear sunglasses to avoid the glare from the lights of film crews. The hearings worked through a roster of what the FBI called "friendly witnesses" during the first few days of the carefully planned testimony. The investigations have been labeled a show trial by critics, and with good reason. The FBI had been working for months to ensure that HUAC had a good supply of potential anti-Communist witnesses. It had also identified possible Communists through eight years of FBI investigation. When the hearings began on October 20, the SDG immediately came into sharp focus with the testimony of the conservative director Sam Wood, who was president of the MPAPAI. Wood argued: "There is a constant effort to get control of the Guild. In fact, there is an effort to get control of all unions and guilds in Hollywood. I think our most serious time was when George Stevens was president; he went in the service and another gentleman took his place, who died, and it was turned over to John Cromwell. Cromwell, with the assistance of three or four others, tried hard to steer us into the Red river, but we had a little too much weight for that." Sam Wood had a gentle-looking face that belied an almost obsessive anti-Communism: he made his children swear anti-Communist affidavits or face being disinherited. He had started his career as an assistant to DeMille in 1915, and these long-time colleagues were now strong anti-Communist allies. Wood had become a respected film-maker in his own right, directing films such as *A Night at the Opera* (1935) and *Goodbye, Mr. Chips* (1939). His failure to win an Academy Award for his often highly successful films fostered enormous personal spite toward liberals whom he felt were out to discredit him. His strident anti-Communism is thought to have contributed to his death by a heart attack in 1949. Wood and other friendly witnesses had one clear message: Communists were present in Hollywood and were working day and night to wrest control of the industry.[7]

The SDG board had established a special committee to investigate the subpoenas and consider their response. Board members George Stevens, John Ford, Merian C. Cooper, John Huston, George Sidney, and William Wyler sent a telegram to Congress protesting that any investigation should be conducted by bodies such as the FBI and the courts. This telegram was part of a broader pattern of initial support across the film industry for those called before HUAC in the first hearings. The directors mentioned in Wood's testimony were incensed. Edward Dmytryk, Irving Pichel, Herbert Biberman, Robert Rossen, and Lewis Milestone protested to HUAC about Wood's testimony, but its head, J. Parnell Thomas, shrugged off these approaches. The group wrote to the SDG president, George Stevens, arguing that Wood's allegations needed to be refuted. It is uncertain whether the SDG board responded to the telegram or acted independently. On October 21, 1947, the SDG board met to consider the issue. After some debate, and against the objections of the director and board member Lesley Selander, who applauded Sam Wood's comments, the board rejected the testimony about Communist activity in the Guild and protested in a telegram to the committee.[8]

After finishing with the anti-Communist witnesses, who included the actors Gary Cooper and Adolphe Menjou and the producer Jack Warner, HUAC then turned to suspected Communists, or "unfriendly witnesses." About nineteen witnesses were called, of whom ten would testify at this opening round. This group would later be known as the Hollywood Ten—the larger group would be called the Hollywood Nineteen. The group included eight writers; two of the directors, Biberman and Dmytryk, were SDG members. The screenwriter John Howard Lawson, who was a prominent figure in the Communist Party in Hollywood, was the first to be called before the committee. Lawson had written the screenplay for *Dynamite* (1929), which was directed by Cecil B. DeMille. His testimony descended into a screaming match. Thomas banged his gavel repeatedly while Lawson yelled at the committee: "I am not on trial here, Mr. Chairman. This committee is on trial here before the American people. . . . It is an invasion of the right of association under the Bill of Rights of this country." He refused to answer questions about Communist Party membership, and officers escorted him away. The hearings were widely broadcast on news features, and the American community saw suspected Communists yelling at a government committee.[9]

The directors fared little better. Biberman had enjoyed a solid career writing and directing pictures such as *King of Chinatown* (1939), *The Master Race* (1944), and *Action in Arabia* (1944). He was also one of the founding members of the SDG. He was born in Philadelphia and educated at Yale and in Europe. He joined the Theater Guild and soon became one of its leading directors. In 1930 he married the actress Gale Sondergaard, who would also later be blacklisted. Looking like a schoolteacher with his clear spectacles, suit, and bow tie, Biberman tried to be more polite and deliver a prepared statement, but he could not compete with the gavel-banging and hectoring of Thomas, who demanded: "Are you now or have you ever been a member of the Communist Party?" Despite his initially quiet demeanor, Biberman began yelling at the committee, pushing his index finger into the desk repeatedly as he tried to make a point. His finger became a fist, pounding the table. His testimony lasted barely a minute.[10]

His fellow director Dmytryk watched the testimony and felt community backing eroding as the proceedings dragged on. At the time of the hearings, Dmytryk was a highly successful director. He had started as an editor before the uncredited directing of *Million Dollar Legs* (1939), which led to a series of low-budget films before he made his breakthrough with a seminal film noir, *Murder, My Sweet* (1944). Not long before the HUAC investigations began, Dmytryk had made a strong film about anti-Semitism called *Crossfire* (1947). Even though it was a modestly budgeted film, it received several Academy Award nominations. Shortly after the film was finished, both Dmytryk and the film's producer, Adrian Scott, were called to testify before HUAC. Scott and Dmytryk had also been a director-producer team on *Murder, My Sweet* and *Cornered* (1945). Like the others, Dmytryk refused to testify. He was able to answer a few questions and claimed HUAC was out to split the SDG. He refused to answer questions about his membership in the Communist Party and was excused by the committee. The remaining subpoenaed SDG members, the directors Lewis Milestone, Irving Pichel, and Robert Rossen, escaped testimony. Milestone and Pichel were not Communist Party members and would eventually be cleared, but their careers were damaged by association. Rossen was a former member and would take the Fifth Amendment defense in 1951 when asked to testify to HUAC. In 1953, suffering poor health and desperate for work, he did testify, naming many Communist members. Among the many people he named were his fellow directors Dmytryk, Frank Tuttle, and Bernard Vorhaus, although by this stage naming names had become a meaningless ritual, as the committee knew every Communist in the film industry.[11]

After each unfriendly witness had refused to testify, his Communist Party affiliations, meetings, and membership cards were displayed. The HUAC investigators then read out a long list of charges and evidence of Communist activities collected by the FBI over the previous six years. The HUAC investigator Louis J. Russell presented the evidence against the directors, saying, "Herbert Biberman is reported to have been a member of the party for approximately 18 years. Edward Dmytryk was issued Communist Party book No. 84961, for the year 1944, and when the party was reportedly dissolved in the summer of 1944 and the Communist

Political Association organized in its stead, he was issued 1944 Communist Political Association membership card No. 46859, and for 1945 the Communist Political Association membership card No. 47238."[12]

The hearings presented a faintly hysterical version of Communist activity in general and of the SDG in particular. In reality the level of Communist involvement in the Guild was fairly low. One of the few Communists in the Guild, Frank Tuttle, would later testify to Congress that the work of the pro-Communist directors in the running of the SDG was not effective. They could really only support liberal candidates and a few of the Party's own members during Guild elections to the board of directors.[13]

The Hollywood Ten were backed by the Committee for the First Amendment, a group consisting of many high-profile figures in Hollywood who went to Washington to protest the hearings. The arrival of prominent actors in support of the unfriendly witnesses created a huge amount of media attention. At first media reporting was tilted in favor of the Hollywood Ten, prompting Thomas to phone the FBI on October 28, 1947, concerned about the editorial coverage. Thomas was focused not only on how the newspapers depicted the hearings but also on his own media profile. During the hearings he even posed for photographs with friendly witnesses, such as the actor Robert Taylor, in an attempt to bolster his own personal publicity. To create even more interest in the press, Thomas fed false rumors to the journalists that a surprise witness would testify to link Hollywood Communists to the theft of atomic weapons. No such evidence emerged. Two days later, HUAC representatives told the FBI that they were running out of funds and the "friendly press" was wearing thin, which meant that it would be difficult to maintain public interest any further. HUAC also believed that it would be a great "psychological move" to discontinue the hearings while the event was still relatively well received. Thomas then shut the hearings down early and proposed no legislation—the ostensible purpose of the inquiry—but instead demanded, "The industry should set about immediately to clean its own house and not wait for public opinion to force it to do so." The day after the inquiry closed, the influential columnist Frank R. Kent wrote that the "plain truth" was that Communists had not been discredited during the proceedings and had made Congress look incompetent.[14]

At this point the hearings appeared to be a failure from the conservative viewpoint, even after the Hollywood Ten were charged with contempt for their refusal to cooperate with the committee. Most of the Hollywood Ten returned to their jobs believing they had scored a victory. Five hundred people greeted the unfriendly witnesses when they arrived back in Los Angeles. However, the celebrations were short-lived: the studios soon fired the unfriendly witnesses, and it became clear that some of their actions—such as Lawson's screaming at the HUAC hearings—had started to alienate allies. The director John Huston, a staunch defender, later argued that he was against "what was being done to the Ten, but [he] also disapproved of their response." Others just abandoned them. The actor Humphrey Bogart, who was a prominent member of the Committee for the First Amendment, was forced to write an article for *Photoplay* magazine saying he was "no Communist" and that he had been duped into supporting the Hollywood Ten. Even though he still called HUAC a "vaudeville" show, he offered no further backing for the Hollywood Ten. Others followed suit. Despite this deteriorating support, some, such as Huston, the screenwriter Philip Dunne, and the director William Wyler, continued to campaign behind the scenes, but their efforts lost momentum and were ultimately abandoned.[15]

The hearings were not popular in industry circles, even among conservatives. The Association of Motion Picture Producers asserted that "Hollywood is weary of being the national whipping boy for Congressional committees. We are tired of having irresponsible charges made again and again and again and not sustained. If we have committed a crime we want to know it. If not, we should not be badgered by Congressional committees." These sentiments were repeated, using the same kind of language, in a speech made by DeMille to the Commonwealth Club in San Francisco on November 7, 1947. He spoke about the rise of Communism and the threat it posed to American cinema, claiming there were Communists in Hollywood who were very dangerous "because they're brainy ones." According to DeMille, the Communists' objective was to destroy free enterprise and free government. He argued that Communists aimed to control the motion picture industry through subtle means, as the industry would not tolerate any propaganda. Yet even DeMille did not give the HUAC investigation his full backing: "Hollywood will not welcome being made a whipping boy for the benefit of headline hunters and sensation seekers or irresponsible mudsmearers." According to press reports: "Commenting on the recent investigation of filmland Communism by the House Un-American Activities Committee, DeMille said he thought Reds were neither more [n]or less active in Hollywood than in other major American cities. . . . 'Hollywood is a convenient target for so-called witch hunters. . . . I sometimes think these hunters are actually hunting headlines while the real witch sits in her little red tent and laughs at them.'" A change took place two weeks later on November 20, when DeMille discussed the issue privately with FBI agent Richard B. Hood. He said that Hollywood would have to clean house and personally committed to introduce a program to remove Communists. He believed "Congress is using the motion picture industry to awaken public opinion to the dangers of Communism." DeMille's reversal was reflective of the entire industry.[16]

Within the SDG, the question of how to deal with the HUAC investigations was generating clear political divisions between conservatives and a more moderate group of directors. This second group had leaders including Ford and Stevens and links to liberals such as Huston, Billy Wilder, and Wyler. It was not particularly well organized and could not be considered to have had any cohesive platform or ideology. Stevens's political outlook was indistinct to those who knew him. Huston later described him as a strong American liberal, and he was staunchly opposed to McCarthyism in all its forms. Ford described Stevens as a conservative; DeMille was never sure. The FBI monitored him, but all the Bureau noted was that he stood for fair play. Stevens was without doubt one of the most influential of the group as a three-time president of the Guild. He was certainly a patriot who had volunteered for duty in the Second World War. He filmed the D-Day landings and the Battle of the Bulge. One of his personality traits was his passive-aggressive style of leadership. He developed a facade of total passivity, never saying a word while being lambasted by a studio executive for issues such as cost overruns. The executive would eventually give up, and Stevens would go on his way, directing the film as he chose. It would be a mistake to think that his soft-spoken demeanor indicated any personal weakness. Working across almost every film genre, Stevens had emerged as a formidable and highly successful director who had triumphed in the studio system over four decades. He was not a man to cross.[17]

Huston and Wyler had been far more vocal in their public opposition to HUAC. With Wilder, all had joined the Committee for the First Amendment. Huston stood six foot two, a larger-than-life figure with a string of affairs and marriages. A top writer of successful films, he had broken through as a director with the success of his film *The Maltese Falcon*

(1941) and then established himself as a writer-director of the first rank when America joined the war. Despite having had childhood illnesses that would have granted him an exemption, Huston volunteered for military service. During the war years he filmed documentaries in the Aleutian Islands before going on to film *The Battle of San Pietro* (1945). This was a reenactment depicting Allied soldiers clearing Germans from the countryside close to a small town near Naples. He returned to Hollywood and resumed his career as a top director. Despite his military service, the FBI concluded that Huston was "associated with Communists," noting that his 1948 film *The Treasure of the Sierra Madre* featured a speech that "was practically a direct quotation from MARX." The film won Huston Academy Awards for directing and writing.[18]

Wyler had given Huston his start as a writer on *A House Divided* (1931), and the two would remain lifelong friends. Wyler had immigrated to the United States in 1921 and had been directing prestigious films since 1925. Like Huston, he volunteered for service in the Second World War. In 1943 Wyler was embedded in the U.S. Army's Eighth Air Force stationed in England, and the director proved himself fearless as a filmmaker, almost losing his life while making a documentary of B-17 bombers in action over Nazi-controlled France and Germany. During this time he directed a documentary about the bombing mission of a B-17, the *Memphis Belle,* which bombed heavily fortified submarine bunkers in Germany. In 1945 he filmed the destruction inflicted on the coast of Italy from an open compartment in a B-25, subjecting himself to a deafening amount of noise, which caused him to lose almost all his hearing through nerve damage. Wyler returned a disabled veteran and used his experiences at war and his homecoming to inform one of his masterpieces, *The Best Years of Our Lives* (1946). This film upset conservatives by its depiction of the callous treatment of returning soldiers. One scene that showed a banker's reluctance to give a soldier a loan was read by some as an attack on capitalism. Wyler was one of the early leaders of the Committee for the First Amendment and its campaign against HUAC. By the time of the investigations, he was one of the most successful film directors in Hollywood, having won the Academy Award for best director for *Mrs. Miniver* (1942) and *The Best Years of Our Lives.*[19]

Often confused with William Wyler was Billy Wilder: the pair would receive compliments for each other's films because of the closeness of their surnames. Wilder was born in Austria and fled Europe with the rise of

Hitler. He was remarkably talented; beginning as a screenwriter in 1929, by 1950 he had established himself as one of the preeminent writer-directors in Hollywood. Wilder was not a joiner. He was a natural cynic and seemed to enjoy attacking almost every political view. *Ninotchka* (1939) is a witty assault on Stalinism, while *Stalag 17* (1953) made all sorts of jabs at informing in the HUAC era. In later years he would attack corporate capitalism in *The Apartment* (1960) and Communism again in *One, Two, Three* (1963). The film he made closest to the time of the SDG meeting, *Sunset Boulevard* (1950), is now regarded as one of the greatest films of American cinema. The film was a brilliant but cynical view of the way Hollywood simply forgot its past. The only survivor in this weird environment was Cecil B. DeMille, playing himself as the veteran director who triumphed where others perished.[20]

As the 1947 hearings took place, this more moderate group held sway in the SDG. However, political tensions rose in the Guild as conservatives closed ranks in support of HUAC. Some of the sniping that took place between the directors focused on their films. During the debate on how to deal with HUAC, John Ford said the only picture he knew of that hinted at Communism was Sam Wood's *For Whom the Bell Tolls* (1943). While Ford made this swipe privately at a board meeting, his opponents had no such qualms. Earlier that year, the Soviet director Sergei Eisenstein had singled out Ford's films *Tobacco Road* (1941) and *The Grapes of Wrath* (1940) for praise. After the publication of Eisenstein's article, just before the HUAC hearings, DeMille highlighted Ford's *Tobacco Road* and Wyler's *The Little Foxes* (1941) as examples of cinema that suited the needs of Communists. DeMille argued that the American people knew that, "with all its faults," capitalism had delivered the highest standard of living and greatest personal freedom. Communists could not deny this fact, but they could "pick the sordid and degraded parts of America" to fool their audience into believing that America is a vast Tobacco Road and successful people are all "little foxes." In contrast to DeMille, his conservative ally Sam Wood defended *The Grapes of Wrath* in his HUAC testimony. He said, "I don't know if they would be anxious to show that picture, because, after all, as poor as they were, they did have a piece of ground, and they did have an automobile, and they are at liberty to get [in] the automobile and travel across the country."[21]

These simmering differences became a power struggle. On November 24, the House of Representatives voted 346 to 17 to cite the Hollywood Ten with contempt. One week later, on December 3, 1947, studio executives signed the Waldorf Statement saying they would remove any employee who would not attest under oath that he or she was not a Communist. The blacklist had begun to operate, and those named on it could not find work in the film industry. The impact of the blacklist on the SDG and other labor organizations was immediate. The Waldorf Statement created a problem for the studio heads: how to develop a mechanism that would vet possible Communists in order to avoid further HUAC investigations. A loyalty oath was one such means as a form of self-policing. The guilds of writers, actors, and directors would be encouraged to purge their members in order to forestall further investigations.

Not all of the Hollywood producers were happy with the Waldorf Statement or the subsequent firings. DeMille would prove pivotal in reversing opposition to the HUAC hearings at two key meetings of producers and directors in December 1947. Walter Wanger complained bitterly about HUAC at the producers' meeting on December 5, 1947, and was building momentum against the committee. DeMille interrupted Wanger, lecturing him that it was neither the time nor the place to attack Congress. Louis B. Mayer defended Wanger and said, "For the first time in my life, I am forced to disagree with Cecil B. DeMille." He went on to complain about his own personal treatment by HUAC. Mayer had been questioned at length about *Mission to Moscow,* which he defended as being a wartime necessity when the Germans were in Stalingrad. DeMille regained control of the debate, saying, "It simply boiled down to whether or not a man was for America or against it, and there is no middle ground." DeMille's words sealed the debate. Studio head Harry Cohn applauded "our hero, Mr DeMille," saying, "C. B. always crashes through when you need him." DeMille had played a crucial role in quieting opposition to the committee at the producer level and backing away from the Waldorf Statement.[22]

DeMille now turned his attention to the SDG. In an act largely overlooked, he successfully proposed a mandatory loyalty oath for all officeholders of the SDG in 1947. Before the meeting, DeMille phoned SDG president George Stevens to discuss the agenda. Stevens said that the agenda was how to deal with the present anti-Communist drive by the producers, and an innocuous invitation to the meeting was sent out. DeMille, joined by his fellow conservatives Sam Wood, Leo McCarey, George Marshall, and David Butler, packed the SDG meeting with people sympathetic to "the American system." The shift in power was immediate. DeMille was seated at the executive table, although he held no position. Robert Rossen urged a protest by the Guild against the firing of Edward Dmytryk, who had also hoped for member assistance in his fight against HUAC. The move was blocked. One of the Hollywood Ten, Herbert Biberman, also tried to offer a countermotion to attack HUAC, but DeMille ruled him out of order, arguing that it was "no place to criticize the Congress of the United States." Wyler attempted to make some remarks and was immediately challenged by DeMille: "Are you pro-American or un-American; That is the only question." Since DeMille had stacked the meeting, the proposals to protest against HUAC's methods and actions were quashed and a motion was presented to introduce an anti-Communist loyalty oath for all office-bearers of the SDG instead. One director asked for a secret ballot on the oath, as no one would dare oppose it openly, but the loyalty oath for officials would be decided on a show of hands. Out of 150 to 200 directors, John Huston claimed only he and Billy Wilder publicly opposed the oath for officials. Michael Curtiz jumped up demanding that their names be taken down for the record. In the middle of the chaotic scene, DeMille rose and started shouting that this was a war.[23]

The successful drive to introduce the oath for SDG office-bearers was ahead of legal developments such as the Taft–Hartley Act, which called for union officials in the United States to sign a loyalty oath. Although the law had been passed on June 23, 1947, the anti-Communist oath had been challenged by the American Communications Association in the U.S. Supreme Court and would not take effect until May 8, 1950. The court eventually ruled that the laws were constitutional. Introducing a measure for officeholders to sign an anti-Communist oath showed an impatience with the slowness of the legal system by DeMille and his allies. This impatience would eventually contribute to his undoing. Despite his outward success, DeMille's tactics at the first loyalty oath meeting had alienated many people in the Guild, and he would later learn that his opponents could organize and defeat him in the same emphatic manner. Some of the anger directed toward him at the later and more famous meeting in 1950 was a result of this earlier takeover of the Guild and the manner in which he won his position. For the moment, the anti-Communists had flexed their muscles in December 1947 and pushed through a loyalty oath for the SDG. Huston was so angry he wanted to turn over a table. The next time he attended a meeting, the general SDG meeting on October 22, 1950, there would be a much different result.[24]

The loyalty oath for SDG officeholders was a show of force by the new anti-Communist group. A far more important move occurred later in the December 1947 meeting when, owing to a by-law that said a board member had to vacate his seat after being absent for three meetings, DeMille and Wood were both elected to the board. This signaled a turning of the political tide at the SDG. John Cromwell would later speak of his frustration that a month after his HUAC hearing "the General Meeting elected to the Board of Directors the man who had made the accusations in Washington against me and which the Board had found utterly unfounded." DeMille reported back to the FBI that "there was no motion made of any kind to support the ten men who are being indicted." One of the FBI informants noted: "As a result of DeMille's 'quarterbacking,' the resolution was passed 115 to 10." In the end DeMille gloated, "That crowd got their thorough licking . . . our crowd swept to power." The SDG was following the path of other labor organizations in Hollywood. On November 21, the Screen Writers Guild election saw twenty of its twenty-one offices delivered into the hands of anti-Communist members. The SAG introduced a loyalty oath for officials in January 1948. Right across all the labor organizations, the conservatives had wrenched power away from liberal defenders of the Hollywood Ten. Even so, the guilds still could not agree on a joint loyalty oath.[25]

At the next SDG board meeting, on January 13, 1948, the conservatives began to demonstrate their influence. Wyler was stopped from removing the conservative Mabel Walker Willebrandt as legal counsel, even with Ford's backing. Willebrandt was a former U.S. assistant attorney general and the highest-ranking woman in President Herbert Hoover's Republican administration; she had been behind the push to have J. Edgar Hoover appointed as director of the Bureau of Investigation—the precursor to the FBI—in 1924. Known as "Prohibition Portia" for her strong and unrelenting legal attacks against bootlegging, she flourished in a male-dominated environment, and her success was so great that she even made the cover of *Time*. Following the election of Franklin D. Roosevelt in 1932, she left the federal government but retained a legal practice in the capital, remaining in contact with Hoover. The FBI noted her letters to its director advising of "the internal affairs of the SDG," in which she reported infiltration by "Communist elements." Like DeMille, Willebrandt was a member of the MPAPAI, and she would become its vice president in 1954. Her legal knowledge, networks, and advocacy at federal levels helped establish the Guild.[26]

DeMille consolidated his new-found authority by conscripting every "reliable anti-Communist" and gaining their proxies for the SDG board elections in March 1948. He enlisted ten people, who each recruited an additional nine people to vote in the board elections. The DeMille group's organization and commitment swept them into the top SDG positions. The veteran director George Marshall, a strong political ally, was elected president to replace Stevens. Brazenly, the new conservative group flaunted their FBI connections. During a debate in which the non-Communists Pichel and Milestone were denying any party membership, Willebrandt bragged about her friendship with Hoover, saying that he was the only person who could decide who was a Communist. The objectives of the newly installed conservative majority on the SDG board were clear and openly stated. In a speech titled "While Rome Burns," delivered to the Economic Club of Detroit, Michigan, in April 1948, DeMille spoke about the individual's role in preventing the spread of Communism. He asked people to spot the "Communists and party liners" in their union ranks, warning that it is "easier to coast along and compromise until we find ourselves in the grip and at the mercy of a red-ruled board of directors." DeMille considered his opponents at the SDG to be Communists, or at least "ensnared liberals" who would be "liquidated" by Communists when they had served their purpose. It appeared, however, that the conservatives had liquidated them first. After a few months of control of the SDG board, DeMille reported that the left was in decline and that he was proud to announce there was "no political discussion and no question of contemporary issues" at the SDG; the "Communists had gone underground."[27]

The conservatives ruled without seeming rancor for the next two years, but there were warning signs. After gaining office at the SDG board, DeMille became its representative on the Motion Picture Industry Council and would become the latter organization's second chairman in February 1949. His appointment was controversial, prompting the Hollywood American Federation of Labor Film Council to withdraw from the MPIC. The Film Council represented several key unions in the industry, including the SAG and the International Alliance of Theatrical Stage Employees. It protested DeMille's appointment because of his "right to work" campaign. The withdrawal of the Film Council struck a massive blow to the image of unity between labor and film management. DeMille dismissed its departure, saying he was elected by the MPIC and would vacate if requested. The issue was minor and attracted only scattered newspaper coverage; however, it was a forewarning of how divisive DeMille's brand of politics could become. Overall, he felt comfortable in his leadership role at the SDG and spoke openly about setting up a conservative political dynasty. It was time, he thought, for a younger man to be trained to assume the conservative mantle. At the height of his influence, DeMille nominated Joseph Mankiewicz for the position of president at the 1950 election.[28]

As DeMille cemented himself at the SDG, the legal battle for the Hollywood Ten was being fought out in the courts. Many supporters of the group believed that the U.S. Supreme Court would overturn their contempt convictions on constitutional grounds, a decision that would bring with it the collapse of the Waldorf Statement. These hopes, however, were dashed when the U.S. Court of Appeals rejected their appeal in June 1949. Fate was against the Ten. In 1949 the liberal justices Frank Murphy and Wiley Rutledge died; it was expected that they would have ruled in favor of the Hollywood Ten. They were replaced by Tom C. Clark and Sherman Minton, who shifted the court to the conservative side. In such a national emergency with the threat of cold war, Clark—a former attorney general in the Truman administration—argued that it was hard to see "how there could be any more pertinent question [of Communist Party membership] in these circumstances." HUAC had the constitutional right to ask people about the membership of political parties. In April 1950 the U.S. Supreme Court refused to hear further appeal, and the Hollywood Ten were sentenced to jail. The imprisonment of the Hollywood Ten for contempt drew a line in the sand. Hollywood would be forced to clean its own house, as J. Parnell Thomas had demanded. The studio executives believed the loyalty oaths would remove the political pressure concerning Communism. The growing blacklist created a climate of suspicion throughout the film industry, as well as opening up one of the bitterest chapters in American cinema history.[29]

2

The Origins of the Screen Directors Guild Meeting

The Red Scare period reached its high-water mark in 1950. After trials lasting two years, former State Department official Alger Hiss was convicted for perjury for his alleged involvement in a Soviet spy ring on January 25, 1950. The case brought former HUAC member Richard Nixon to national prominence. On February 9, 1950, Senator Joseph McCarthy declared at a speech in Wheeling, West Virginia, that there were 205 card-carrying members of the Communist Party in the State Department. Even though the senator was a late arrival on the anti-Communist scene, the sheer viciousness and near hysteria of his anti-Communist campaign would designate the period the McCarthyite era.[1]

The political temperature was certainly on the rise in Hollywood. The Waldorf Statement, and even the imprisonment of the Hollywood Ten, did not end demands for stronger anti-Communist intervention. In May 1950 John Wayne, in his role as president of the Motion Picture Alliance, called for a complete delousing of the film industry. "Let us, in Hollywood, not be afraid to use the DDT," he told newspapers. The blacklist created by the Waldorf Statement was only part of the equation. More corrosively, people could be put on a "graylist"—a list of those who were not Communists but were believed to have Communist sympathies. These people also could not obtain work. On June 22, 1950, the American Business Consultants published a report titled *Red Channels,* listing 151 names of show business figures accused of Communist ties, including many in the film industry. The editors openly stated they were not interested in whether people actually were Communists, and the evidence presented was often fragmentary or simply incorrect. Even so, those who appeared in such a publication required a political clearance in order to return to work. The clearance process was haphazard, and people with no Communist connections could lose their livelihood. The Waldorf Statement had created within the film industry a toxic work environment, in which any self-styled patriotic organization could label any producer, actor, director, or writer a Communist and jeopardize his or her career. To heighten matters, on June 25, 1950, North Korea invaded South Korea—the Cold War had become hot.[2]

In response to the growing tensions, the Motion Picture Industry Council (MPIC) tried to unite all parts of the industry, both labor and management, in a common front against Communism. This was partly a public relations initiative to present an image of an industry pulling together to put the past behind it. Loyalty oaths were a key part of the response to HUAC and a means of settling things down in the industry. President Harry S. Truman had already introduced loyalty oaths for federal employees on March 21, 1947, and institutions across the country—notably many universities—followed suit. DeMille was a strong supporter of the loyalty oath. He wrote to HUAC after Truman's announcement saying that all industries, including the film industry, should follow the president's example: "The standards set up by the President could well be applied by . . . schools, labor unions, civic organizations, and by employers in nationally vital industries that mold public thought." By October 1950 the MPIC was poised to introduce such an oath, negotiating an industry-wide agreement on the controversial issue. Its adoption, at least at the SDG, appeared to be a foregone conclusion.[3]

To secure the oath for all members, DeMille convened a special emergency meeting of the SDG board on August 18, 1950. The aim was to draft a new by-law making a non-Communist oath compulsory for present and future members. It is often assumed that DeMille exploited Joseph Mankiewicz's absence (he was in France for a holiday) to move forward with the mandatory loyalty oath. The timing may have been a coincidence. DeMille already had control of the board and could push through dubious measures against the strenuous objections of Mankiewicz, John Ford, and others. Power at the SDG rested with its fifteen-member board; the president did not even have a vote unless there was a tie. DeMille's actions suggest that he assumed Mankiewicz's support; indeed, the president's name was attached to the notice announcing the loyalty oath, even though he had no knowledge of the initiative.[4]

Mankiewicz was not the only person unaware of the board's decision. Frank Capra was also listed as a signatory, and he had not attended the

August 18 meeting. Capra and DeMille were close political allies. Capra always portrayed himself as the grateful immigrant from Sicily thrilled with the opportunities for fulfillment presented by the United States. He had risen from humble origins to become a venerated director and a president of the SDG. Capra was also a lifelong Republican who served at times as an FBI informer and would join DeMille in moving against Mankiewicz. Despite his political leanings, Capra directed many films with a distinct liberal edge. Movies such as *Mr. Deeds Goes to Town* (1936), *Mr. Smith Goes to Washington* (1939), and *Meet John Doe* (1941) featured ordinary people pitted against the rich and powerful. *It's a Wonderful Life* (1946) was singled out by Ayn Rand in her analysis for the FBI as a film with anticapitalist messages. Capra's documentary *The Battle of Russia* (1943), part of the wartime propaganda *Why We Fight* series, also caught the attention of conservatives with its heroic depiction of Soviet troops. Capra would initially support DeMille in his campaign for a loyalty oath and against Mankiewicz. In time, he would reject both positions.[5]

DeMille later argued that he had acted with some urgency because a large group of directors in New York—almost certainly from the rival Radio and Television Directors Guild (RTDG)—planned to join the SDG, but they would do so only provided there was no Communist taint in the organization. Even at the time, this claim was weak; DeMille's own report to the FBI mentions a group of New York directors planning to join the Guild and the loyalty oath, but no link was made between the two developments. The claim was not baseless, however: some conservative New York directors may have preferred to join the SDG because the alternative RTDG was decidedly more progressive in its outlook. The Guild's relations with its radio and television rival were poor at that point, especially as the RTDG was about to charge the SDG with undue employer influence before the National Labor Relations Board. The subsequent hearings were bitterly fought, with Mabel Walker Willebrandt labeling the RTDG as "Communist dominated." Taking her case a step farther, Willebrandt wrote to Hoover on September 21, 1950, pointing out that the RTDG president, Richard Mack, was living with an unmarried woman and accusing the unnamed woman of having had five abortions and of freely dispensing her "physical favors" to radio stars.[6]

DeMille's real motives were openly stated. It was a matter of pride for DeMille that the SDG be the first guild to introduce a mandatory loyalty oath and for the action to ripple through the film industry and beyond. He believed that, in signing the loyalty oath, the Guild was sending a clear message to Communist sympathizers: you were either on the American side or on the side of traitors and fellow travelers. After the August 18 vote was tabulated, the SDG board stated, "We are confident that other workers, in our own and other industries, will step in line with us, closing the ranks of loyal Americans united for the ultimate victory and lasting peace in a world purged of Communist tyranny and aggression." The MPIC and other guilds were still making faltering steps toward an anti-Communist oath, but DeMille saw himself as a leader who was forging ahead.[7]

At the August 18 meeting, the SDG board authorized an open and signed ballot to be sent by mail to members for endorsement of the loyalty oath. In theory this open and signed ballot would allow DeMille to record the names of his political opponents. The ballot was passed 574 to 14. DeMille confidently reported to his FBI contact that the SDG membership had given its own mandatory oath about 85 percent support, and that all members would "execute the non-Communist oath," now and in the future. Given the general intimidating atmosphere, the result of the vote was not surprising. However, some directors were alarmed that the by-law had been pushed through with an open ballot, particularly while Mankiewicz was out of the country. One director, Fred Zinnemann, had refused to vote on the oath; when he received a reminder to do so, he still refused and was cabled by the SDG board to complete the ballot. He protested in writing that the open and signed ballot was a coercive way of voting used only in dictatorships. Zinnemann had arrived in Hollywood in 1929 from his native Poland, but he had grown up in Austria and saw similarities between the Red Scare in the United States and the growth of fascism in Europe. In time Zinnemann would become one of Hollywood's premier directors, known for films such as *High Noon* (1952), often read as an allegory of McCarthyism. But in 1950 he had only just broken through with *The Search* (1948), after struggling to establish himself for some years in the American film industry. Even so, Zinnemann felt compelled to make a stand.[8]

Upon returning to the United States on August 23, 1950, Mankiewicz was confronted with this small but growing dispute within the SDG. Journalists showed him copies of newspapers telling him that the board had pushed through a non-Communist loyalty oath, supported by the vote of the membership. Initially, he made no public comments about the oath. With official approval, he eventually circulated a statement that he had been unaware of the action taken by the board and would make a full announcement upon returning to Hollywood. Even after gaining board approval for this statement, however, Mankiewicz was taken to task for "criticizing the action of the Board of Directors and Membership," and he was contacted by Vice President Al Rogell, who told him to make no further public announcements.[9]

After returning to Los Angeles, Mankiewicz chaired the next board meeting on September 5, 1950. Here the growing political tensions erupted, with Mankiewicz showing he could be a formidable character. According to one observer, while Mankiewicz was usually placid at board meetings, in this instance he shouted down his opponents. The argument in the meeting centered on the "vehemence of the members who were questioning the manner in which the oath was adopted, and its compulsory nature." Although the ballot had passed 574 to 14, Mankiewicz felt there was greater discontent and that the real position was in "sharp variance to the outward picture of unanimity painted by the astronomical percentages of the open ballot vote." He challenged the move, saying the open ballot was a flawed system. However, he then backtracked and conceded that the by-law was in place and therefore there was no point in debating the issue further. He focused his energies on the proposal that the membership should be invited to a general meeting where it could be informed about the implications of signing or not signing the anti-Communist oath. As president, Mankiewicz was not able to vote, but he could still use his position to question Willebrandt about how the by-law would operate. She confirmed that by refusing to sign, people could be expelled from the Guild and denied work. Mankiewicz argued that the Taft–Hartley Act, which placed clear restrictions on unions, made it compulsory for union leaders to sign the oath, but the same regulations did not apply to the general membership. The oath now contained a clause—Article X—which designated who was in "good standing" as a Guild member and therefore employable. Three lists were going to be constructed: one for those categorized as in good standing; one for those ineligible owing to their failure to pay dues; and one for those "not in good standing"—that is, "not recommended for employment by reason of having not signed a non-Communist affidavit." The new by-laws were approved subject to a final draft.[10]

Opponents of DeMille and Willebrandt were starting to demand firmer action against the mandatory loyalty oath. Mankiewicz would later argue that he turned down several requests from a group of directors who wanted a general meeting. He may have resisted these calls, but his own public statements were becoming more critical. On September 14, 1950, a few days after the board meeting, Mankiewicz traveled to New York to accept a B'nai B'rith award for his work in upholding the American democratic ideal. In his speech Mankiewicz made references to the HUAC investigations and other references that almost certainly applied to DeMille and his group. He said the American liberal did not accept groups or individuals that set themselves up as legal tribunals and that threatened to deprive people of their protection under the law and possibly their livelihood. DeMille was not to be diverted. On September 27, 1950, workers at Paramount Studios gathered to sign a "declaration of freedom," which sounded suspiciously close to a studio loyalty oath, and DeMille praised the assembled workers for standing up against "the black reaction of the Kremlin."[11]

The debate within the SDG was becoming increasingly shrill, but with the oath and various by-laws now in place, the dispute appeared essentially academic. Yet at the October 9 board meeting there was further and even more strident debate. The sticking point now was that the SDG was going to send a list of those directors who had not signed the oath to the producers. The list would give information on the directors' political status to their employers. Mankiewicz would later recount, "To my knowledge, no other guild, union or group of professional and creative men had ever issued such a list of their members to prospective employers." Although DeMille still controlled the board, support for his hard measures was beginning to erode. One board member—almost certainly John Ford—said he was "fed up with all the controversy about oaths in general" and he wanted to return to the business of focusing on the professional needs of directors.[12]

At this same meeting, Mankiewicz also spoke up; he felt answerable to the disgruntled Zinnemann faction. He told DeMille, "I do not know how much longer we can keep this business of a tight little Board of Directors sitting on a membership who have a lot of questions to ask." Mankiewicz insisted that he was not attacking the by-law, which had been duly passed, but that he was upset with the open and signed system of balloting. He said, "Until Russia and Moscow concur, the open ballot will never reflect democracy of a group of men in public." Referring to the by-law as a "blacklist" prompted a furious response from DeMille and his supporters. Mankiewicz argued that this term was justified, as they had a new by-law "which states specifically lists to be sent to the producers, one in good standing and one not in good standing because of the oath."[13]

The debate became heated, and the transcribers had difficulty keeping up. At one point Mankiewicz shouted that he would not sign the oath, setting off a train of events that would result in his attempted recall. Ford also objected to the oath, saying his business colleague Merian Cooper would refuse to sign it too. Ford could not see the point of the oath and was getting frustrated with the whole debate. He continued, "Things are tough enough. Why send it to the producers?" Ford's main aim was to "better our own standing as directors," rather than to better the Guild's relationship with the producers: "What [have] I helped organize this Guild for? . . . I am against a police state as much as Communism." Other board members rebutted him, saying, "We do not say they cannot work by this statement. The producers can make their own decision and hire him." Despite Ford opposing the measure, DeMille retained majority board support and successfully moved that the new measure for the oath was passed.[14]

Technically, the proponents of the by-law were correct: producers could employ a member who had not signed the oath. However, given the poisonous political atmosphere, it was unlikely that any producer would have employed a director who had not signed; therefore, directors who did not sign the loyalty oath would find themselves on a blacklist. The membership lists also undermined DeMille's central argument that the aim of the non-Communist oath was to recruit the New York directors. The whole thrust of the oath was to identify any potential Communists and report them to producers. In the midst of the debate, a compromise was reached. A revised single "not in good standing" list of members was to be established. The reason for a name appearing on this second list could be nonpayment of dues or it could be failure to sign the oath, but this time, "the reason for lack of good standing would be furnished to the producer upon inquiry." After a long debate, this compromise position was agreed on by the board.[15]

Mankiewicz insisted on calling a general membership meeting to discuss the ballot. He told DeMille that he was apprehensive about the future of the Guild and that its unanimity was at stake. He announced that he would call a meeting in ten days' time and possibly step down if that was what the members wished, saying, "Either I represent the membership or I do not represent, I have got to have that clarified once and for all." He said the membership deserved "the benefit of the democratic approach" and this general meeting would dispel this "dissension." Mankiewicz argued that the membership had elected him, so it would be the membership who "[would] decide." He would ask the membership to choose between the viewpoints of DeMille and himself. To calm the tension, the board members reassured Mankiewicz that they wanted him to remain president. They also reiterated that they did not want a general meeting, owing to "their determination to avoid open disunity at any costs." After this fractious board meeting, Ford talked privately to Mankiewicz and persuaded him not to hold the general membership meeting. Throughout the SDG upheaval, Ford would continue to play the role of peacemaker between the warring factions.[16]

One of the most remarkable aspects of the SDG general meeting that was eventually held on October 22, 1950, was that it never needed to happen. After vigorous debate at a board meeting, the by-law—with the blacklist provision—became part of the rules and regulations of the Guild. Mankiewicz withdrew his threat to call a general meeting, and the matter appeared to have been resolved. Even on a personal level, things calmed down. DeMille told Mankiewicz that he respected his position as the Guild president who was fighting for what he thought was right. According to Capra, "[DeMille] reminded the President that he nominated him for the office and would do so again." While political and personal tensions had increased within the Guild, DeMille had been successful in having his changes implemented. Almost the entire membership had endorsed the by-law, and it was passed by the board with some small compromises. In the simplest and plainest terms, DeMille had won. Yet, in an incredible display of self-destructive behavior, he snatched defeat from the jaws of victory.[17]

Two days after the October board meeting, this delicate power balance in the Guild was upended. An article appeared in *Daily Variety* reporting that Mankiewicz refused to sign the loyalty oath and would lead a revolt within the SDG. The DeMille faction was furious over this account, particularly its references to a "bitter debate" about the oath, and immediately concluded that Mankiewicz had leaked information to the media. DeMille convened a meeting of supporters at his Paramount offices and began moves to recall—or remove—Mankiewicz from his position as president. The recall group met at 6:00 p.m. on Wednesday, October 11, 1950. Ford and Stevens were renowned for never missing a meeting, but they were not present at this gathering. Reportedly, prospective Mankiewicz supporters such as Stevens received telegrams notifying them of the meeting as late as 6:30 p.m. The group was convinced that the media article foreshadowed an all-out attack on the board. After his outburst about blacklists at the board meeting, they could see no other option than to recall him.[18]

Details of the meeting are sketchy, but according to DeMille's ally John S. Waters the call did not originate from DeMille. The recall may not have been DeMille's idea, but he gave it his full support. The strategy involved a ballot that, if signed by 60 percent of the membership, would result in the president losing his position. The SDG's executive secretary, Vernon Keays, was told to be at the office at 7:30 the following morning. Keays worked all day and well into the night with SDG staff to print and distribute the ballots to recall Mankiewicz's presidency. The names of fifty to fifty-five possible Mankiewicz supporters were left off the recall mailing list intentionally, to stack the vote and avoid any countermoves to stop the ballot. The recall ballot offered a choice of either voting "Yes" to Mankiewicz's removal or not voting at all. Motorcycle couriers delivered the ballots up until 3:00 a.m. on Friday, a move later described by John Huston as "a putsch in the night." The politics of the SDG had turned ugly.[19]

The reality was that Mankiewicz had no plans to mount an attack on the board and had accepted his loyalty oath defeat. It was not he who had leaked the *Variety* story, and the recall group was reacting to a nonexistent threat. As one member of the recall committee, Frank Capra, later observed, "Many assumed that Mankiewicz had given *Variety* the story. The assumption was wrong. That was the recall committee's great mistake. . . . Conversely, Joe [Mankiewicz] was wrong in not calling up some board members to deny the story. That, too, would have stopped any recall movement."[20]

The recall ballot was a major blunder, as there was no justification given for the dismissal. Directors began to demand information from the recall committee about what was going on. Realizing their mistake, the DeMille group sent out a telegram to justify the recall. Delivered to directors on October 13, 1950, the telegram stated: "Mr Mankiewicz has . . . pitted himself against the legal governing body of the Guild, its Board of Directors. He repudiates the democratic vote of its membership. He stands with 14 against 547." It was signed by eleven of the fifteen board members, plus four additional directors who had been added to the recall committee to give the impression that the whole board was united against Mankiewicz. These four extra directors were Henry King, Leo McCarey, Lesley

Selander—who was a second vice president and not on the board—and Andrew Stone. Those board members who did not sign the telegram were George Stevens, John Ford, Claude Binyon, Merian C. Cooper, Walter Lang, Frank Borzage, and George Sidney (there were alternate directors).[21]

Despite the fumbling efforts of the recall group to keep the ballot away from him, Mankiewicz received a copy from his fellow director H. C. Potter, and one was even mailed to his address. Mankiewicz contacted the lawyer Martin Gang, who suggested two immediate actions: a legal injunction to stop the ballot, and a petition for a general membership meeting. John Huston sponsored the injunction, and Mankiewicz's supporters gathered at Chasen's restaurant on the evening of Friday, October 13, 1950. The supporters needed and gained twenty-five signatures on a petition to call a general meeting. Those signing represented a cross section of Hollywood politics and personalities. They included some of the more outspoken members of the Committee for the First Amendment such as Wyler and Huston. Some of the signatories, such as Joseph Losey, would later face blacklisting. The petitioners included young directors who were just beginning their careers, such as Robert Parrish and Richard Brooks. Jean Negulesco was normally apolitical; his main link to the petitioners was his friendship with Huston. A few of the signatories, such as John Farrow, were considered "reactionaries" by the liberal left in Hollywood. Don Hartman had been an ally of Ronald Reagan's on the Hollywood Independent Citizens Committee of the Arts, Sciences and Professions, where he opposed people such as Dalton Trumbo; he was also proud of his role in driving out the left in the Screen Writers Guild, and he was about to be promoted to head of production at Paramount Studios. While they did not sign, George Stevens and Elia Kazan sent proxies in support.[22]

The diversity of this group was an ominous sign for DeMille; it showed that he was burning bridges with some key colleagues and political allies. While the petitioners held no common political viewpoint, they were united in at least one resolve: to protest against DeMille's actions. Even so, the political environment made them fearful of retribution. Brooks remembered business agents warning their directors of the consequences of signing the petition, particularly those who had recently immigrated and were not yet American citizens. He later said people actually wept from fear. The stakes were high: many of the petitioners felt that their careers were on the line. To forestall any allegations of their own Communism, all the petitioners also signed the loyalty oath.[23]

The Mankiewicz group found it difficult to register its petition as the SDG offices were closed when they arrived on a Saturday. They suspected the collusion of Executive Secretary Keays, since a meeting could not be called without his involvement. DeMille and Keays were long-time associates, having both worked at Paramount Studios since the 1920s. In fact, the office never opened on the weekend, and the anti-recall petitions were delivered on the following Monday, October 16, 1950. Mankiewicz later apologized for suggesting that Keays obstructed the delivery of the petition by closing the office on the weekend. He was not apologetic about the fact that the petitioners could not obtain a membership list to present their case straight to directors. Unable to gain a membership list, the Mankiewicz supporters began telephoning members to ask them not to sign their recall ballots. Later that day, the issue was presented to the Los Angeles Superior Court with the SDG's legal counsel, Mabel Walker Willebrandt, agreeing that no recall ballots would be counted until after the projected meeting. Willebrandt also agreed that the pro-Mankiewicz group could gain access to a membership list.[24]

While the debate continued in directorial circles, the board met once more, on Wednesday, October 18, 1950, to supposedly decide on the proxy form to be used at the meeting. Ford used the opportunity to try to avoid a general meeting. As a first step the controversial practice of open ballots was scrapped. Mankiewicz, who had by now signed the new loyalty oath, produced a letter from *Variety* editor Joe Schoenfeld attesting that he had not been the source of the disputed article—the root cause of the recall movement. Ford spoke forcefully that the Guild should concern itself with professional matters. The board, containing a majority of fifteen members of the recall committee, then gave Mankiewicz a fresh vote of confidence. At the same time, the Assistant Directors Council, which was affiliated to the Guild, also gave Mankiewicz a unanimous vote of support. The divide was nearly bridged. One of the recall committee members, Frank Capra, drafted a letter to praise Mankiewicz for signing the oath, believing this act would definitely end the recall campaign.[25]

All that was required was for DeMille and the recall committee to rescind the recall motion. It is not clear why the October 22, 1950, meeting did proceed, given the level of support for Mankiewicz, but DeMille asked for an agreed joint statement from Mankiewicz, who refused, saying the wording was unacceptable. In a later interview Mankiewicz said that DeMille's demands were excessive, as Mankiewicz was expected to offer public penitence. The first draft for a telegram from Capra was certainly heavy handed, talking about "thought control" and Mankiewicz abiding by the rules. However, Capra revised the draft to make it a straightforward compromise: "Representatives of the Recall Committee have met with Mr Mankiewicz and settled their differences. The Recall Committee withdraws its proposal for the recall of Mr Mankiewicz and requests the Board of Directors to destroy all recall ballots without count or tabulation of the number of ballots or signers of the same. Mr Mankiewicz reaffirms his acceptance of the by-law requiring a non-Communist oath, as evidenced by his signature of the said oath on October 13th. The members of the Recall Committee endorse the vote of confidence given Mr Mankiewicz by the Board of Directors on October 18th." Capra claimed it was accepted by Mankiewicz and all it needed was DeMille's approval. It was checked off by several recall committee members, such as Tay Garnett, Henry King, Frank McDonald, George Marshall, Al Rogell, William Seiter, Andrew Stone, and John S. Waters. Other options were also presented, suggesting the proposed joint statement went through several drafts.[26]

DeMille and Mankiewicz would later feud over the failure of an agreed joint statement, but neither side's stance makes any real sense. Perhaps a clearer insight into the breakdown of civility is provided by Capra, who wrote the next day: "At the board meeting that night, called for the technical purpose of approving the form of proxy to be used at the general meeting, it became obvious to me that the original issue of whether or not the Guild should require a loyalty oath from its members, was completely forgotten. Instead, it was clashing personalities, personal vindications, control of the Guild, lefts, rights, closed offices, accusations." Capra resigned from the board in protest when the recall of Mankiewicz was not scrapped, disgusted at the general behavior of all concerned. The initial debate about a loyalty oath and open ballots had descended into a power struggle. This point was made clear when Mankiewicz told journalists he wanted to wrench dominance away from a tiny group within the board and return democratic control to the members.[27]

It should have been clear to DeMille that his support was crumbling. Before the celebrated meeting, George Sidney called DeMille on October 21, 1950, anxious to speak to him. Perhaps now best known for his musicals, Sidney was one of the most respected and popular members of the Guild, and DeMille had even chosen him to replace Huston on a key SDG committee that would seek to end leftist influence. His cinematic anti-

Communist credentials were demonstrated when he directed *The Red Danube* (1949), a film that presents the Soviet Union in bleak terms, focusing on the plight of a daughter of Soviet dissidents. He was a political ally of DeMille's and would remain a strong supporter of the anti-Communist oath for years to come. Sidney would be elected president of the Guild in 1951, succeeding Mankiewicz, and he would hold this position for fourteen of the next sixteen years. He had already sounded out DeMille's close business associate Donald Hayne about the possibility of DeMille resigning from the board and had been told DeMille had no interest in taking such a drastic step. Relieved, he encouraged DeMille to stand firm, adding that he hoped no one would have to resign. The approach, intended to be diplomatic, indicated how precarious DeMille's position had become, even among his allies.[28]

By now it was DeMille's position on the line, not Mankiewicz's. DeMille's drive for a compulsory loyalty oath in the film industry was also falling apart. The MPIC, watching the events at the SDG from a distance, ditched their own plans for a compulsory loyalty oath, favoring an idea of the Screen Actors Guild to develop a voluntary version. The SAG hoped to use a voluntary oath as a mechanism to tackle claims raised by publications such as *Red Channels*; it thought the oath should be voluntary so it could never be used for a blacklist.[29]

Still, nothing was left to chance by either camp. George Stevens and the lawyer Martin Gang interviewed all the staff at the Guild office, with Stevens emerging from the investigations claiming that there was enough evidence to seriously damage DeMille. Along with Stevens's investigation, a group consisting of Mankiewicz, Huston, Stevens, H. C. Potter, and Wyler met daily to plan for the meeting. On the other side of the political fence, DeMille's speech was written by Hayne, who was his speechwriter and would later edit the director's autobiography. DeMille went over the speech painstakingly, making diagonal marks on the page to indicate dramatic pauses and underlining passages that he wanted to highlight. He made a few changes in pencil, only moderating some of the political language. Despite DeMille's marked ability to organize meetings and stack them with his supporters, he was facing a strong challenge, as this meeting was in front of the entire membership. DeMille would need to perform at his absolute best if he wanted to succeed—or even survive.[30]

3

The Screen Directors Guild Meeting

It is fitting that one of the most famous meetings in Hollywood history was convened in an architectural icon: the Beverly Hills Hotel. The hotel was erected in 1912, before the area was even officially founded as a city. Dubbed the Pink Palace, it was the city's first historic landmark. Its ornate crystal room, which had been created during a renovation in 1947, was already a major venue for debutante balls. The Screen Directors Guild needed a venue of that size to make room for the five hundred assistant and senior, or full, directors who crowded into the space on the evening of October 22, 1950. Under the strict rules of the Guild, all members were permitted to speak, but only the senior directors could vote. Given the gravity of the events, a stenographer, Marion Farrell, recorded every word spoken over the next six hours. Even amid all the acrimony, Joseph Mankiewicz introduced the session by noting the death of the director Christy Cabanne at the age of sixty-two on October 15 and reading an obituary. For those looking for omens, this was not a good portent for Cecil B. DeMille. Cabanne had been an assistant director for D. W. Griffith and had embarked on a career as a director in 1913, about the same time as DeMille, continuing to work until two years before his death. Mankiewicz called for pallbearers for the upcoming funeral for the silent film director, screenwriter, and actor, and then the meeting began in earnest.[1]

Mankiewicz's Opening Speech

Mankiewicz shared the stage with the entire board, including DeMille. Even though it was a Sunday night, the room was packed and journalists hovered outside the doors. Mankiewicz opened the formal proceedings at

43

8:00 p.m., citing one objective: "that when we close this meeting, the Screen Directors' Guild of America will emerge more than ever before a united Guild." He called on speakers to express themselves politely, saying, "This meeting can become very easily the most important in our history. It is entirely up to us whether we shall remember this night with satisfaction and pride or whether it shall be remembered as the night we lost the Guild." His own introductory remarks certainly were diplomatic, as he described in a factual manner the events leading up to the meeting. He refused to name people involved in the dispute and even referred to board members as "board member one" and "board member two" when reading from minutes. He identified people only if it was impossible to do otherwise; for example, he named Mabel Walker Willebrandt as the legal counsel as that was her office alone—but he apologized for doing so.[2]

Mankiewicz recounted that while he was in Europe, he received a series of telegrams from the Guild officers advising him of Guild business, with no mention of the prospect of a mandatory oath. A normal SDG meeting was conducted on August 14, but the minutes were not forwarded to him. He received a telegram on August 16 from Al Rogell saying all was going well. When he left France for the United States on August 17, he was unaware that a special emergency meeting of the SDG board had been called just the day before. On arriving back in New York on August 23, he received telegrams from SDG members about the loyalty oath decision saying they had signed the ballot out of "expediency and fear," and "only one or two voted no." None opposed the oath, but all of them questioned the compulsory aspect of the decision: "Most of the members who protested by wire and telephone against the manner in which the oath had been adopted had voted 'yes' on the ballot." Mankiewicz was approached by journalists who demanded, "'Why the emergency?' . . . 'Why since the Taft–Hartley Act demanded a loyalty oath only of Guild officers and directors, why was the Screen Directors' Guild making it compulsory to its membership as well? Had any other professional Guild or Union ever done it?'" He felt ill-equipped to answer these questions and issued a holding statement. He seemed stung by the criticism from the recall committee that he had attacked "the action of the Board of Directors and Membership." He pointed out that he had prepared his statements with the assistance of the SDG press relations counselor Carl Post, who had shown them to the board.[3]

After returning to Hollywood, Mankiewicz attended the next meeting of the SDG board on September 5. Here he learned what he believed to be the real impetus for the oath: "It was repeated to me . . . that another essential reason for our emergency action was the desire to be the first of the Hollywood Guilds and Unions to make a non-Communist oath mandatory upon its membership." Mankiewicz then detailed his discussions with the board, particularly his efforts to ensure that members understood the impact of not signing the oath. He pointed out that the New York group of directors had not left their union; no other Guild had undertaken such a drastic step, and none had yet followed the SDG. He told the board, "We have a duty toward the membership that we should face—let's answer some questions the members want to ask. . . . I would like very much to think that this Board thought enough of its membership to make clear that part of the new by-law as it affects his right to work." ("Right to work" was a phrase used frequently by DeMille in his campaign against the American Federation of Radio Artists imposing a one-dollar levy.) Despite opposing the loyalty oath himself, Mankiewicz argued, "The by-law has been passed by the Board of Directors and voted by the guild—there is no point in debating it."[4]

Mankiewicz positioned himself as a president who had disagreed with the actions of the board but who had worked assiduously to calm fears and concerns about the oath. He also spoke about opposing the penalty by-law at the October 9 meeting, and the concern of a growing number of members about the board's high-handedness. Again he repeated, "I find . . . another instance in which I tried to make clear again that I had no intention of attacking a by-law which had been passed." Even so, he saw the changes involving the loyalty oath as enabling a blacklist: "I want to make it clear that I did refer to the separate list of members 'not in good standing by reason of non-compliance with the non-Communist affidavit and not recommended for employment' as a black list." In the heat of the moment, he had said he would not sign the loyalty oath, he admitted. It was a flash of anger in a tense meeting. He pointed out that he had signed the same oath three times as a board member. After the October 9 meeting, Mankiewicz had wanted to summon a general membership meeting to discuss the implications of the loyalty oath, but he was persuaded not to do so by John Ford—whom he did not name. He was disappointed to read the headline in the next issue of *Variety:* "Mankiewicz Will Not Sign Oath." He denied any role in the article, again citing an affidavit from the *Daily Variety* editor Joseph Schoenfeld that supported the denial. Briefly dropping his civility, Mankiewicz admitted his anger over the recall petition: "The nature of

45

it, the manner in which it was launched, and the politburo quality of its instigation was so foreign to everything I have ever known or learned or thought as an American, that I prefer not to include in this report any of the details of which I have since become aware." Mankiewicz mentioned the role of his supporters who had contested the recall, if only to "express my gratitude to all of you for it."[5]

Following Mankiewicz, Al Rogell, the SDG vice president, then formally read out the affidavit that had instigated the recall. Rogell was a thin man with thick black hair. He had been a director of westerns since the 1920s and would soon move over to TV. Photos of him on the film set often show him goofing around with actors; one such image depicts him playing checkers with the actor Ken Maynard on the back of his horse, Tarzan. He did not seem comfortable in this spotlight, however, and kept to a short, prepared legalistic statement. After being contacted by a group of New York directors, the board had moved to introduce the oath. It was the New York directors, he explained, who had requested such a step. He said the open ballot had been a standard practice for the Guild. Despite being interrupted, Rogell insisted "that the affiant [a person who swears to an affidavit] verily believes as do many other members of the Guild that the continued public utterances of said Joseph Mankiewicz are giving a false impression of the Guild . . . [and is] seeking the recall of Joseph Mankiewicz of the Guild in conformity with legally adopted rules of the Guild."[6]

DeMille Takes the Floor

Cecil B. DeMille was then invited to respond to Mankiewicz. A spotlight cast a glow on DeMille's bald head as he spread the pages of his speech on the speaker's table. He began in an amicable manner, congratulating Mankiewicz on his "splendid presentation of events that have led to an unfortunate but not an irreparable situation." He spoke for himself, he explained, and not the board: "I was at every meeting at which this matter was discussed, and I have come before you neither to praise Caesar [n]or to bury him." By paraphrasing a quote from Shakespeare's *Julius Caesar,* he possibly hoped to repeat Mark Antony's famous role in reversing an angry mob's fury and regaining their support. "There is nothing I want from the Guild," he expounded. "There is nothing the Guild can give me. I do not seek any office, nor would I accept any office. I have been here with many of you. I see Dick [L'Estrange] . . . over there who was in it thirty-eight years ago, and my race is nearing its end." (A former bank clerk and vaudeville performer, L'Estrange had appeared in a role in *The Squaw Man* [1914], one of the first feature films made entirely in Hollywood, which was codirected by DeMille.) DeMille reminded the directors that he was one of the pioneers of the industry. He had nothing to gain but the "welfare of this body. . . . Whatever I say here has only one object—that is to settle the differences that are endangering the life of this Guild."[7]

The board had given Mankiewicz a vote of confidence, but DeMille wanted to clarify a few points. Turning to the recall, DeMille admitted that it was "sheer stupidity" to fail to send out a membership-wide telegram explaining the recall ballot. Most members simply received the ballot with no context or explanation—many late at night. In a rare admission of fault, DeMille said, "I was one of the men who sent it." He wanted to settle the matter once and for all because "the Guild, as Mr Mankiewicz has said, cannot serve its purpose when it is torn apart by dissension, [if its] . . . selected leaders refuse to execute the expressed will of the majority." This is a curious statement. The meeting's transcript reads "selected" leaders, but an "elected" leader makes more sense, and the word "elected" is in DeMille's original speech. It may have been a simple transcription error, or it could have been a Freudian slip on DeMille's part, since it was he who had nominated Mankiewicz for president in the first place. DeMille then argued that the elected leaders could not refuse to execute the expressed will of the majority, and "a willful minority" could not be "permitted to use the Guild as a sounding board or a battering ram for their own devious and ulterior purposes." This minority—almost certainly those people DeMille considered to be Communists—were referred to ambiguously at several points in his speech.[8]

DeMille signaled his willingness to end the fight: "We have had enough of charges and counter-charges. No progress, I believe, can be made by continuing to hit each other on the head, because it does not, or perhaps it will not feel so good when we stop." DeMille repeated the claim that the impetus for the loyalty oath was an offer by thirty-four New York directors to join the SDG as long as it did not brook Communists. Rogell had received a message on August 16, and a meeting was immediately convened in response. He reminded the directors that the president was only a presiding officer without a vote, unless there was a tie. The board had every right and the power to enact substantive changes to its by-laws. He stood by the board's action in sending out a signed and open ballot, which gave every member the opportunity to vote on the oath before it was adopted. He graciously referred to the petitioners as "twenty-five or thirty sensitive, honorable, good Americans who feel there is no necessity to sign such papers." (The entire membership had voted 547 to 14 in favor of the measure.) He rejected Mankiewicz's charge that the whole vote was an election in the style of Russia—a "ya" ballot (on which people are able to vote yes or not at all). "If this does not mean that Mr. Mankiewicz thinks the members of this Guild lack the courage of their convictions, then what does it mean?" he questioned. DeMille then asked, would the 547 members "who voted openly for this oath . . . have voted against it if it had been secret? Is Mr. Mankiewicz accusing the 547 of his fellow members or any of them of . . . [craven cowardice]?"[9]

The move to recall Mankiewicz stemmed from his accusations about a blacklist and his own purported refusal to sign the loyalty oath. DeMille said that at the October 9, 1950, board meeting Mankiewicz had wielded the word "blacklist" at least five times. DeMille repeated that the board had no intention of authorizing a blacklist and insisted that the Taft–Hartley Act protected people whether they signed the oath or not: "Any producer is free to hire any director who refuses to take a Guild oath." He argued, "The only purpose of the oath is to give assurance to the men who joined this Guild that they are joining a clean organization." This is another interesting comment: DeMille spoke of men who "joined," not men who were considering joining, suggesting the focus was also on the present membership, not the prospective recruits from New York.[10]

DeMille conceded that comments in a heated meeting can lead to people putting things more strongly than intended. DeMille was applauded when he described the SDG board as a group of "good American men . . . who are tough fighters, and believe me Mr Mankiewicz is a tough fighter. . . . We thought he meant what he said." He continued, "No one has accused Mr Mankiewicz of being a Communist. When I nominated him for President of this Guild, I thought he was a good American, and I still think he is a good American." DeMille went on to say Mankiewicz had every right to oppose the by-law and refuse to take the oath, but in doing so he could not occupy the office of president and "cast forth damaging accusations at its Board of Directors and its members." He argued that this had been the sole reason for the campaign to recall Mankiewicz.[11]

DeMille dismissed ideas that the media played a role: "The Recall

Committee did not need to look in the press. It only needed to look in the minutes to which I refer you for every one of the factual statements and quotations I have made." It was an unconvincing argument, when one considers that DeMille launched the recall drive shortly after the *Variety* article appeared. DeMille contradicted himself further when he referred to "damaging accusations" and said that the press had had a "field day."[12]

Putting aside the flaws in his argument, DeMille had begun well: he was conciliatory toward Mankiewicz and his case was coherent. It was a difficult meeting in which he was under enormous personal pressure, yet his remarks had attracted strong applause. Any nominal support he had mustered, however, began to evaporate when he started reading out a list of leftist organizations, which the twenty-five directors supporting the Mankiewicz petition were either members of or associated with in some way: "Then a strange thing happened. Suddenly there appeared on the evening of Friday the 13th, a group of twenty-five gentlemen [who] gathered in a restaurant to do battle for Mr. Mankiewicz. . . . One of them was Chairman of a testimonial dinner for the Hollywood Ten." DeMille went on to mention others who were on the Committee for the First Amendment, the board of the Actors Lab, the Committee of Arts, Sciences and Professions, and its predecessor, the Hollywood Democratic Committee. One was a known sponsor of the Hollywood League for Democratic Action, while other signatories belonged to the Freedom from Fear Committee and the defunct League of American Writers' School. All these organizations had been labeled as Communist or Communist fronts over the past few years by the Tenney Committee or others. He concluded, "Troubled waters attract strange . . . [fishermen] sometimes. I am making no accusations against anybody least of all Mr Mankiewicz."[13]

Even though DeMille deliberately chose to speak only about the political affiliations of the "twenty-five gentlemen" in general terms, in the existing political circumstances he was effectively slapping a label on them: Communists. DeMille's assistant director and supporter Eddie Salven looked on in horror as people began heckling; he sensed the room turning against DeMille. The meeting was now in uproar. Despite the noise, DeMille plowed on: "What is their object? Is it to protect . . . [an injured] Mr. Mankiewicz?" DeMille argued that the group of twenty-five who opposed the recall was "heavily loaded with the elements that have been repudiated by this Guild in election after election and vote after vote." The people in the pro-Mankiewicz group were fine individuals, he added, but the organizations to which they belonged may have been taking advantage of them. Watching from the front row, with hand cupped around his ear to compensate for his deafness, William Wyler saw it in a different light, believing that DeMille had just branded him and the group of anti-recall signatories as traitors. He remained silent for the moment but seethed with anger. It was not only what DeMille had said; it was the way he said it. Both Vincent Sherman and John Cromwell would later note the tone in DeMille's voice with its insinuating message.[14]

DeMille believed the issue was a power struggle between the conservatives and their foes, all of whom had demonstrable links to Communism: "Is it their object to split this Guild wide open so that the *Daily Worker* and *Pravda* can gloat over the spectacle? Do they want to widen the breach between the President and the Board until members of the Board will resign and leave the door open for these repudiated elements to return to power?" DeMille predicted that the success of the anti-recall group would lead to the Guild's death, calling on members to close ranks against a common enemy. Then, perhaps sensing that his support was slipping away, DeMille departed from his prepared speech and again noted that some of his opponents were "splendid American citizens." But Mankiewicz received one parting shot: DeMille concluded by saying that the meeting was unnecessary and could have been prevented if Mankiewicz had put his name to the joint statement approved by the recall committee, "a statement which could have avoided this laundering of rather soiled linen tonight." He somewhat confusingly added, "I recognize that Mr. Mankiewicz has now signed the oath which he didn't have to sign because he had already signed it." DeMille finished by saying he always believed Mankiewicz was a "loyal American," that his recall should be closed and all ballots destroyed. The only differences among the factions now were over "questions of procedure." This conciliatory gesture was met with applause. DeMille's motion to terminate the recall was seconded by George Sidney.[15]

DeMille had put a brave face on his performance, but it was a clear defeat. Even though the recall had been formally stopped and he had backed down, the meeting had a long way to run. The debate between Mankiewicz and DeMille had only underlined the political reality that the attempt to recall Mankiewicz's presidency had already failed. DeMille thought that his motion would resolve the dispute and end the meeting, but he could not have been more wrong.

Reaction to DeMille's Speech

DeMille's speech, particularly his linking of directors in the Mankiewicz group to leftist organizations, had antagonized many in the room. One after the other, directors stood to denounce DeMille. The first was John Cromwell, a former SDG president (1945–1946), who had already felt the venom of the anti-Communists when Sam Wood testified to the House Un-American Activities Committee in 1947 about him driving the SDG into a "Red river." He was not a Communist, but he would be blacklisted in 1951. While president of the SDG Cromwell had antagonized studio heads. He had even received a demand for an apology from Jack Warner on October 15, 1945, for the SDG's claim that Warner had hired strike-breakers. Cromwell was also one of many directors who refused to work on *I Married a Communist* (1949), which was renamed *The Woman on Pier 13,* a political litmus test by RKO producer Howard Hughes. This was more than enough for him to be called a Communist. Such sketchy allegations would eventually destroy his career as a director. Despite the serious and looming threat to his livelihood, Cromwell was not afraid of DeMille and did not temper his criticism in his short statement: "All I would like to say is that you made a very earnest statement, and I took it as a request that the important thing before this Guild was unity. Therefore I must say I am astounded at the acrimonious accusations, the unfounded accusations of Mr. DeMille." Cromwell was applauded when he asked how this statement constituted "an effort to retain the unity of the Guild." DeMille responded that he was quoting from the Un-American Activities Committee of the Legislature in California reports of 1947, 1948, and 1949—the Tenney Committee. Cromwell replied sharply: "I think this membership should be asked if they accept the authority of the Un-American Activities Committee of this state."[16]

One of the pro-Mankiewicz signatories, Don Hartman, took the floor next. At the age of fifty, he had thick curly hair that had begun to recede into a widow's peak. Hartman could be funny and charming. He was a writer of successful comedies, such as the "Road" movies with Bob Hope and Bing Crosby, and had recently graduated to directing. Hartman could also use his humor to devastating effect. DeMille had chosen to stigmatize his opponents as left-wing, but he had selected the wrong man in Hartman.

Introducing himself as a vice president of the Screen Writers Guild who had recently been elected against a left ticket, Hartman said he did not like being pushed around by "either the right or the left." He continued: "I belonged to a couple of those organizations. That is fearful and indecent, that anyone has to stand up today with a red, white and blue paper hat and blow a horn and say, 'I am an American.'" Hartman ridiculed DeMille's loyalty oath: "It is a very sad commentary of our times that it is necessary today for decent people, because the house next door is robbed, to sign a paper . . . saying, 'I am not a burglar.' The only outcome of this [is that they] will be rounded up by police and they will sign affidavits that they are not burglars. That is how silly this is becoming." He resented "paper hat patriots" who had signed the oath, who declared themselves good Americans by their oath making. He condemned the use of the open ballot, calling it silly and idiotic and comparing it to the open balloting of the election process in East Germany: "As far as I know in the history of my life and my family's life, I know of not one thing—and no one knows of one thing—done, which was unpatriotic." He was applauded when he finished by comparing DeMille to other anti-Communist zealots in accusing the signatories of Communism. The fact that a known conservative such as Hartman supported Mankiewicz and now openly attacked DeMille suggested the underlying strength of the anger.[17]

Another signatory, George Seaton, spoke next. Seaton had begun as a writer in the 1930s for films such as the Marx Brothers' *A Day at the Races* (1937) before becoming a director. Although a moderate liberal, he had worked closely with the newly elected conservative board of the Screen Writers Guild and had served as vice president in 1947 and as president in 1948. Clearly annoyed with DeMille's depiction of the signatories as left-wing, Seaton sarcastically reminded DeMille that he too was a member of the Hollywood Writers Mobilization along with "the well known Communist, Mr. John Farrow"—a pointed barb, since Farrow was a strong conservative. The Mobilization developed scripts for shows entertaining soldiers overseas. When he found that Communists were sprinkled among the organization, Seaton resigned from it. He had recently written and directed *The Big Lift* (1950), a film with a strong anti-Communist message dealing with the Berlin airlift. He spoke about his research for this film, and of being held by the Communists for fifty-six hours on a dirty train with his wife and daughter after attempting to enter Berlin. Seaton was applauded when he quoted the organizer of the airlift, General Lucius D. Clay, who said that if we "resort to totalitarianism to defeat totalitarianism we have lost our democratic soul by doing it." Shifting his focus back to the SDG, Seaton lambasted DeMille for going to the Producers Association president, Frank Freeman, for support. DeMille had reportedly said, "I thought you would be interested in what went on at the Board meeting last night"; Freeman told him, "C. B., Joe Mankiewicz is no more a Communist than you are." DeMille was criticized by Seaton for discussing Guild business with the producers. No charge could be more serious for a Guild stalwart. Seaton's speech was met with applause that was so loud Mankiewicz told the audience to keep it "relatively American."[18]

The opening salvo had come mostly from directors who should have been politically aligned with DeMille, undermining his central argument that he was being opposed by leftists. The next speaker was the most wounding yet. William "Wild Bill" Wellman, who was a founding member of the Guild, spoke from the heart, and his opinions carried weight. Apologizing to the actor and director Ida Lupino and a few other women present for his language, Wellman let loose. He called the divided meeting the "God damndest thing I have ever seen in my life, and in my estimation the sides—and it is a horrible expression to use because this is not the thing I thought the Guild was for, but I am not going to mention sides or Communists or anything else, nor am I going to mention signing Communistic pledges. I will sign the God damn thing every five minutes, but that is me, and I am not ashamed of it at all." Taking a pot shot at Hartman, Wellman said:

> If anyone says I am wearing a red, white and blue flag on my head because I say that, I am still all right. That is my own personal feeling, but when I see two factions fighting as these two are and hear the things and know that a guy I am very proud of and very fond of has resigned because he can't stand it any longer, and I don't think he would mind my mentioning his name—his name is Capra—if I were an officer in the Guild now I can assure you that I would be right along with him.

Wellman directly addressed the unfairness of the recall attempt: "I think whenever anyone is elected a President to take care of things and then someone does something without him knowing about it, that is being impolite. . . . Let Mr Mankiewicz stay as President. He is a good guy. He is very capable." Wellman called on DeMille to work with Mankiewicz "for the sake of the Guild" and to concentrate on issues such as directorial credits. It was a short but powerful speech, and Wellman was clapped as he sat down. DeMille had framed the debate about the politics of the participants, but even supporters of the loyalty oath were more concerned with the fairness of the recall.[19]

The next speaker was far more political and focused. Michael Gordon had been one of the first directors to sign the anti-recall petition. A director of well-crafted films including *Cyrano de Bergerac* (1950), Gordon was certainly one of the implied targets of DeMille's speech. The notes DeMille carried to the meeting contained a litany of Gordon's political flaws. He served on the executive board of the politically active theater company Actors' Laboratory Inc. and on the Committee for the First Amendment. He had been an assistant to one of the Hollywood Nineteen, Irving Pichel, as a teacher in the League of American Writers' School screenwriting classes. From 1935 to 1940 he had been a member of the Group Theater, which was considered to be a Communist front—many of its members would be called before HUAC. Indeed, in 1951 Gordon would be named before HUAC as a Communist and would not work in the industry for eight years as a result. Gordon spoke only briefly, complaining that he deeply resented "a meeting that was called for the purpose of preserving the President in office being called a meeting to disrupt the Guild." He too was showered with applause.[20]

Then Herbert Leeds, a journeyman who had directed and edited films since 1932, rose to deliver a long and wandering monologue about Communism, fellow travelers, and Jewish Communist front organizations. He said Guild disunity helped the Communists, and that he had checked out Mankiewicz and found he was "pretty clean." Mankiewicz politely acknowledged this endorsement and moved the meeting on. Leeds was followed by John Huston, who read out an account from the *New York Times* to support Mankiewicz's interpretation of events. The transcriber did not record his reading, but she resumed when he spoke briefly. Huston had planned his comments carefully, thinking and rewriting his short address again and again in the run-up to the meeting. His military record gave his remarks, aimed at DeMille, a vicious sting: "In your tabulation of the twenty-five at the restaurant the other night . . . [h]ow many were in uniform when you were wrapping yourself in the flag?" This remarkably wounding comment would be quoted—or misquoted—by some of the directors present more than thirty years later. Huston's verbal jab prompted

Mankiewicz to try to get the directors to return to discussing the topic of open balloting, but he had little impact, and the rage against DeMille continued.[21]

Following Huston was Delmer Daves, who described himself as Republican, although his most recent films, such as *Broken Arrow* (1950), were decidedly liberal. Indeed, the film's scenarist was Albert Maltz, one of the Hollywood Ten, who wrote the script using Michael Blankfort as a front. (If Daves had known about the use of a front, he could have faced blacklisting himself.) Daves was a close associate of George Stevens's, and the pair were strongly against the recall. They had earlier confronted Vernon Keays, the SDG executive secretary, about his collusion with the DeMille faction. Daves began, "I did not sign the petition. I wish I had. I am a Republican too, Mr DeMille. . . . I resent beyond belief the things that you said as you summarized the twenty-five men." Daves said he agreed with Wellman about the basic unfairness of the campaign. When he had received a phone call about recalling Mankiewicz, he told the caller he wanted to hear Mankiewicz's side of the story. Looking up at the board members sitting on the dais, Daves said:

All of us here look before us and see seated at this Board of Directors table dear friends, and the men who signed this telegram are some of my very dearest friends in this town. Mabel [Walker Willebrandt] is a very dear friend of mine. I can go right down the list. Some of them their kids play with my kids. We are as close as people can be, and I love a lot of people sitting at the table. This has nothing to do with personal acrimony at all, nor toward the men who signed the recall. It merely has to do with the faction and the attack that was made . . . [in] what I consider a completely undemocratic manner, and one which was so secretive by nature that I was shocked. . . . The next thing I knew I received a ballot, and it said, "This is a ballot to recall Joe Mankiewicz. Sign here—yes." There was nothing more. It was not yes and no. I was more deeply shocked.[22]

Perhaps drawing on his distant legal training at Stanford University, where he graduated as a lawyer but never had the opportunity to use the degree, Daves then presented damning evidence against DeMille. He said the recall committee deliberately misled the membership by pretending to be acting on behalf of the entire SDG board, asserting, "[Mankiewicz] is not a personal friend of mine. I am fighting for him here, because I feel our rights and our freedom have been violently hit by what has happened." He discussed the telegram that appeared to be mailed from the board of directors in support of the recall: "It said twelve times, 'The Board of Directors this,' and 'The Board of Directors that.'" Daves called the exercise "an abuse of the privileges of our Guild."[23]

Mankiewicz was passed a note saying that some directors were leaving the room to provide updates to the journalists milling around outside the room. He was furious: "Now, good God, gentlemen, can't we act like adult men? When you go home . . . tomorrow, remember that America is created on the system of sitting around an old stove in the grocery store and talking things over, and then going in a booth and voting the way you feel. Now we are here to talk. Let's talk and let's mind our own business." He then called on another of the anti-recall signatories, H. C. Potter, to speak. Henry Codman Potter was known for films such as *The Story of Vernon and Irene Castle* (1939), *Second Chorus* (1940), and *Mr. Blandings Builds His Dream House* (1948). He had studied drama at Yale University before carving out his career in the cinema. Describing himself as an SDG member older than DeMille and also "an American, as good as Mr DeMille," Potter demanded an inquiry into the "shameful thing of the recall." It was another short speech, but it was the first such demand for an investigation of the recall faction, which would grow louder as the meeting progressed.[24]

Mankiewicz again tried to get speakers to focus on the ballot, which was the formal motion before the meeting. He had a little more success with the next speaker, George Sidney, a board member who told his fellow directors that he had missed the October 9 meeting. Before this meeting, Sidney had told DeMille to stand firm, but now even he was moving from that stance. "Tonight when I . . . said I wanted to be heard [it was] because I didn't like to be in the position of nobody knowing what I said or what I thought. As I told Joe, as far as all the statements in the New York papers and back and forth, if it were true, I think it all got very rough. As far as the recall telegram is concerned, I told the other gentlemen I thought it unfounded and untrue the things that were stated in there."

Sidney believed that Mankiewicz was always fully in compliance with the board, but he took issue with the way the petition group had acted. He said:

I also took exception to the twenty-five men who brought a lawyer from the outside in to ask for a meeting. . . . Mr Mankiewicz mentioned earlier today I proposed a motion that we change our By-Laws so that we have a secret ballot. . . . We have all been emotional here tonight. We all have lots and lots to say about it. I am afraid we are getting far afield from what is in everyone's heart. I know everyone here wants to keep this organization together. This organization has come through a couple of rough years. They have a new basic agreement signed when no other organization or no other group got it. And now I think we should stick to the resolution that is at hand and just fight to keep our group together.

Sidney tried to be balanced in his address, but even he was not supportive of DeMille. The attacks were now coming from all quarters, and no one stood to defend DeMille or his role. Seaton and Potter had been signatories to the anti-recall petition, so perhaps their positions had been expected; Daves, however, was a friend of Willebrandt's and a close associate and friend of many of the conservative directors on the board.[25]

Sidney's more balanced approach was not enough to calm things down. Seaton rose again on a point of order to remind people of the reasons behind the meeting and to explain why the petition group called in a lawyer: "Unfortunately this recall went out late Thursday night. I think the messengers were out at two or three in the morning knocking on doors. We met Friday as soon as we could. The Guild wasn't open on Saturday. We could not present the petition. We tried to figure out a way, because if by Sunday sixty per cent of the membership had voted for recalling President Mankiewicz, he would no longer be president. We could do no other than to take legal recourse." Mankiewicz added that the lawyer had been necessary to file an injunction, but not to call the meeting. Sidney tried to cut in, but Seaton reminded him that they had no option. Mankiewicz ended the debate saying, "The time to quibble on the words is when the members are forced to get a lawyer to get a legal injunction to stop a recall that had gone out. They were prohibited from stopping it in any other way."[26]

Stevens Resigns and the Attack on DeMille Strengthens

Feeling was running strongly against DeMille by the time George Stevens, three-time president of the SDG, addressed the membership. He was carrying a large number of papers and apologized to the audience for sitting down at a table while he addressed his fellow directors. Over the previous few days, Stevens and the lawyer Martin Gang had interviewed SDG staff to find out exactly what had happened. In an announcement that shocked the room, Stevens began by saying he was going to join Capra in resigning from the board: "One thing I am very unhappy to do is to have to make the usual qualification about oneself in regard to their Americanism, etc. It seems necessary. I signed the first non-Communist affidavit when I was President of this Guild in 1948." He followed his resignation with a withering assault: "Mr Mankiewicz's recall was done in such a manner that no Board member that wasn't part of it could find out anything about it. It was rigged, and it was organized, and it was supposed to work. And, gentlemen, it hasn't." Stevens then summarized in detail the various irregularities of the recall, including the removal of fifty-five names from the mailing list and the missing membership lists, which Robert Aldrich, an Assistant Directors Council board member, could not access when a request was made. Stevens accused "a group of members of the Board, not the Board . . . [who aimed] to get Mankiewicz out quick, overnight, or in thirty-six hours, if you please." The group exploited the Guild resources and staff "to get the President out of there instead of informing him." He labeled the recall a conspiracy: "If there hadn't been a slip-up somewhere, or if the integrity of the membership of this Guild, each individual member of this Guild toward himself hadn't frustrated that recall, Mr Mankiewicz would have been out and nobody would have had to clear him and say he was a good American. He would have just been smeared and out." Stevens outlined his reason for quitting the board: "I am off this Board as soon as I can get my resignation to the President. . . . You have heard this talk about goodwill, cohesion, pull together in a Guild. . . . It is not because of anything the Communists have done that I am going off the Board." He accused the board of being focused more on Communism than on defending the rights of directors: "I am going off the Board because I think there are other people in the Guild who appear to be against Communism, or say they are, that are trying to split up this Guild." Taking on DeMille directly, he said, "If you say that this business of twenty-five members petitioning to keep Mankiewicz from being kicked out before the membership can be heard is a Communistic attempt because they want to split it up, suppose they hadn't done anything and Mankiewicz went out[?]" He concluded, "I resigned a Presidency in 1942 or 1943 . . . because the United

States was at war. I believe in defending my country. I did not believe in just saying a word here at the Board table about it." Looking at the transcript in later years, Mankiewicz wrote in the margin that this was "the coup de grâce."[27]

Stevens's opening speech represented the moment when DeMille lost any remote chance of controlling the meeting. Universally respected in the Guild, Stevens had served in the Second World War at the age of forty, producing documentaries on the allied invasion of Europe. DeMille had never served in the military, so Stevens's comments were a sharp rebuke. Stevens had reinforced Huston's remark that the men DeMille was attacking had served honorably in the military, and no less Hartman's jibe of "paper hat patriots." His resignation from the board was telling. Still, DeMille persisted, rising to defend himself on a "point of privilege," objecting to the word "conspiracy." He read out a list of the group of members, arguing that it "is not a committee that would be guilty of a conspiracy in anything but the interests of this Guild." Stevens replied that even the members of the recall committee did not know the full story and pointed to two directors, Clarence Brown and Frank Capra, who had abandoned the group after facts about Mankiewicz's recall had come to light. The audience gave Stevens a standing ovation; Robert Parrish later observed that only John Ford and some DeMille supporters did not rise to their feet.[28]

DeMille, clearly wishing the meeting to be over, pushed for his motion to destroy the recall ballots to be put to the vote. This effort to rescind the recall ballot failed on a technicality, as a by-law stated that an SDG general meeting could not stop the recall once it had been initiated by some members. A new motion that the membership instruct the board to destroy the ballots was proposed by Huston and seconded by DeMille. The discussion then meandered through several topics. Fritz Lang asked about the expenses involved in the recall campaign. He was assured by Leo McCarey and DeMille that all relevant costs had been paid by the recall committee. McCarey, who had been DeMille's ally on the board, admitted that the recall leaders had acted in haste. In an odd apology McCarey said, "It was a fire, and maybe we used the wrong nozzle," and Mankiewicz replied that, be that as it may, he was "the only one that got wet." McCarey said he did not want any more in-fighting, and Mankiewicz immediately retracted his wisecrack. McCarey was a staunch anti-Communist and had joined Wood in testifying to HUAC in October 1947. He had directed *Going My Way* (1944) and *The Bells of St. Mary's* (1945), very popular films starring Bing

Crosby as the progressive priest Father O'Malley. McCarey told HUAC his films were not successful in Russia because they contained God. He wanted Hollywood to produce anti-Communist films as it had done against fascism in the Second World War. In 1952 McCarey would direct one of the more feverish anti-Communist films, *My Son John*—the final political messages of which were fashioned by DeMille. Even hard-core supporters of DeMille were backing off from the fight. The meeting finally voted to destroy the recall ballots with a resounding "aye" and none opposed.[29]

Even though the recall was now a dead issue, the resignation of George Stevens had shocked the room. Rouben Mamoulian rose to remind directors that when the SDG was formed, many people considered the organization to be made up of "red, left, revolutionaries." Mamoulian had a reputation for beautifully crafted films such as *Dr. Jekyll and Mr. Hyde* (1931), *Queen Christina* (1933), and *The Mark of Zorro* (1940). His political views were less certain. Mamoulian had traveled to Rome as a guest of the fascist government in 1937. He was also one of the Guild's fifteen founding members. With his thick glasses, he looked like a gentle man, but Mamoulian was known as being strong-willed. Despite his reputation, he confessed to being nervous, but said events were forcing him to speak. He averred, "It seems to me the very heart of the matter is of course we live in times of great anxiety, and we are apt to get very excited and emotional and all of that is most understand[able]." Born in Georgia in 1897, when it was part of the Russian Empire, Mamoulian said that for the first time he felt apologetic about his accent. He spoke about his great pride in coming to America: "I came here, and I am a Naturalized citizen. A man is born. He has no choice. . . . I wanted to be an American." This was greeted with applause. He continued, "I don't believe in talking too much about Americanism. The work I have done in this country glorifies the country and shows my love for it better than any words can do."

Mamoulian said that he was horrified by what he had observed at the meeting: "I cannot believe my ears when I hear that George Stevens is resigning from the Board. . . . But I cannot see this meeting being dismissed without George Stevens remaining on the Board, because if he resigns, I know what it means." Again his words were met by applause. Mamoulian said it had been a privilege to work with George Stevens, and "that man must remain if we are to sleep at night and not feel that something is terribly wrong with our organization." He then turned his attention to DeMille: "I have known Mr DeMille for a long time. . . . He has always been most cordial to me. . . . [But] I think it is wrong for a member of the Guild within the family to accuse anyone even anonymously without actual data or actual direct knowledge, because it is that that suddenly sows seeds of a terrific mistrust, fear and anxiety and suspicion." More applause was showered on him when he called on DeMille to declare his faith in the members of the Guild. DeMille remained silent.[30]

The meeting veered off course when Executive Secretary Keays took to the floor to defend himself from charges of undue involvement in the recall conspiracy. No one seemed interested in his claims, and his statement made little impact. George Sidney tried to reassert some control over the meeting and proposed a motion that the board reject the resignations of Stevens and Capra, but the attention quickly shifted back to DeMille and his recall group. While Mamoulian was polite in his criticism, the debate turned harsher. William Keighley, well regarded for his gangster films during his tenure at Warner Brothers in the 1930s, said that the charges were so serious it was clear that "there are rotten apples in the barrel on the Board of Directors." He repeated the call for an investigation of the "under-handed work" that had prompted two board members to resign. The meeting passed a motion by acclaim for Capra and Stevens to reconsider their resignations. It was still not enough for some participants. Don Hartman now insisted that DeMille rescind his slurs against the twenty-five signatories: "Since he said he is interested in the unity of the Guild, and since he said he has nothing to gain from the Guild and is interested in fair play, which is the American tradition, in all fair play he should retract what he said about the twenty-five signers who signed in good faith to ask for this meeting."[31]

DeMille responded unapologetically: "I named the number and the organizations to which they belonged. That, as I say, is a matter of record in the Capitol. That is not guess-work or hearsay. And the members seem to have admitted membership in those organizations, whether they may have gotten out of them or not, but I also said that there were many fine Americans on that committee." Then he seemed to contradict himself, saying, "I have only heard those who apparently belong to some of these organizations complain about my suggestion." An SDG member, possibly the montage director Peter Ballbusch, interjected, saying, "Mr DeMille, I don't belong to any of them. I signed it."[32] Responding to this comment, DeMille defended himself: "I would like to say that there were good friends of mine on that committee of twenty-five, and that [there] were good Americans on that committee. Then, I named the organizations to which some of them belonged. One of those organizations is listed as subversive by the Attorney General of the United States. One is declared to be in the [Tenney] Report, the Voice of the Communist Party, etc. So these violent attacks have been going against me, I don't know whether they are a smoke-screen to cover the issue or not." DeMille's words simply inflamed matters. Ballbusch countered, "By association and insinuation, you have accused everyone," and DeMille replied that he was "a little astounded that the attack has turned completely against me." He said he could not retract his statements because they were factual.[33]

DeMille's opponents would have none of it. John Cromwell spoke up: "I hate to take up your time, believe me, because I sit here squirming at all this emotionalism that is going on, and I certainly thought I wasn't going to get into it, but it is pertinent to the point, and it is only this: I [w]as probably the star member of this organization, I wasn't accused in any statement of the committee. I was accused in the National Capitol." Cromwell spoke about his pride in the SDG for standing up to HUAC in 1947 and defending his good name. He confessed his horror at seeing Wood and DeMille elected to the board one month later. Cromwell talked about how he had worked hard to keep political schisms from hurting the board when he was Guild president:

And I only want to point out that when those political considerations were brought into this organization and by whom, and now Mr DeMille gets up and says, "As a matter of record," I wasn't interested in the matter of record. I know about that. They are on the record all right, but I was more interested in the tone of his voice when he made those accusations here tonight, meaning that he meant them, and he believed that those members were Communists or they were in this organization trying to disrupt it. . . . You have heard the most extraordinary accusations brought by probably the soundest, most honest members of this whole organization, Mr George Stevens. Let's get at those accusations and find out whether they are true or not. I for one believe that they are.

Cromwell was cheered as he returned to his seat.[34]

The assistant director Robert Aldrich was next. Aldrich would become a prominent director with films such as *Kiss Me Deadly* (1955), *The Big Knife* (1955), *What Ever Happened to Baby Jane?* (1962), and *Hush . . . Hush, Sweet Charlotte* (1964). At the time of the meeting, DeMille was convinced that William Wyler was trying to hand the Guild over to left-wing leadership by supporting people like the left-liberal Aldrich in the Assistant Directors Council. In his FBI report DeMille promised to either split off the assistant directors from the main Guild or remove the Communist element. Aldrich added to the growing list of accusations against DeMille, outlining how the membership lists disappeared when he sought them as an SDG official. In contrast, the recall committee, with no official status, had access to the lists and to the work of staff. When he challenged Keays on these matters, Keays gave the noncommittal reply that he welcomed any investigation of his actions.[35]

Don Hartman asked for punitive measures: "Mr DeMille, I have charges against you and I would like to put them before the meeting. You now go further. You now say if anyone speaks in his defense it is proof of his guilt. When you speak in your defense that is not proof of your guilt. . . . I accuse you of misconduct in the Guild, and I ask for your resignation." The directors broke into applause. DeMille refused to resign, however, insisting he had made no untoward insinuations against anyone: "I am not accusing anyone of anything. The facts are on the record. I am not accusing them. The State of California did this. I didn't. I made no charges." Hartman's reaction was to formally move that DeMille resign from the board. This motion was quickly seconded by two people: John Cromwell and Ralph Ceder—the latter known for his silent-era comedy shorts. Mankiewicz asked Willebrandt to clarify whether the membership could ask a board member to resign. She replied that the recall provisions that spurred this meeting applied equally to DeMille—60 percent of the membership could vote him out.[36]

Hartman again moved for DeMille's recall, and this time Vincent Sherman formally seconded his motion. Sherman was a liberal Democrat who had been active in organizations such as the Federal Theater Project in New York before coming to Hollywood. He was well regarded as a "women's director" and for the versatility he had demonstrated with *The Hard Way* (1943), *Nora Prentiss* (1947), *The Unfaithful* (1947), *Backfire* (1950), and *The Damned Don't Cry* (1950). In later years he ran afoul of the blacklist when he refused to drop Nedrick Young from the credits of a script under consideration for filming. Young was under HUAC investigation and was later blacklisted. Because of his support for Young and his ties to some antifascist causes, Sherman found himself placed on the graylist. Sherman did not flinch from attacking DeMille directly: "He didn't mention names. . . . The only reason you mentioned the names would be to discredit those men who signed or cast aspersions on them because they were of a color that protested the recall of Mr. Mankiewicz." DeMille blustered that he had not linked people to specific organizations. Sherman replied:

> You referred to them as belonging. There was a purpose in your mentioning those people as belonging to certain organizations. I would like to add one other thing. I have not yet signed the loyalty oath. I am not a Communist. I never have been. I never intend to be. Had this thing been handled democratically, had the membership been given respect and [been] called in to discuss this thing, I would have been the first to sign it. And if it is voluntary, I will right now sign it immediately. I don't like to be pushed around, and I don't like to be told what I have to do. I don't think it is right. To me the whole thing has been a disrespect for the membership, a lack of faith in the intelligence of the membership. That is why the whole thing happened in the first place.[37]

Once again Mankiewicz tried to limit discussion only to the motion. It was clear that the tide had turned against DeMille; sensing the hostility, Arthur Jacobson, the president of the Assistant Directors Council, stood up to throw the main target a lifeline. Jacobson had a long association with DeMille at Paramount dating back to 1929. He told the assemblage, "If tomorrow morning in the press it comes out that Mr Cecil B. DeMille was asked to resign from the Board of Directors, what are we achieving? Mr DeMille, I plead with you, sir, with just a few well chosen words from you, you can clean this up. I just plead with you, sir." DeMille did not take this opportunity to apologize. Another of DeMille's assistants, Eddie Salven, said later that he felt DeMille had missed a real opportunity to calm things down. Hartman again pressed his case, and the motion was to be voted on.[38]

A few called for calm and contrition. The French-born director Bretaigne Windust spoke about the people who had been damaged by the furor, particularly Mankiewicz, and declared it was time to admit that a mistake had been made. The assistant director Morris R. Abrams spoke about the need for unity and said there was no real cause for people to resign: "I think that Mr DeMille and all the rest of the gentlemen of the Board who were elected by the membership have a trusteeship. You are accountable to us, and if mistakes have been made apologies should be made. I make apologies for any mistakes I make."

Al Rogell interjected, furious with George Stevens's claims of a conspiracy; he demanded to call out the names of those who had signed the recall, which he had listed on a document. Mankiewicz called him out of order, but Rogell refused to be silenced, saying that DeMille was only one of the many who had signed the petition. Hartman said he was not charging DeMille of having signed the recall petition, but of making accusations without evidence. Rogell submitted his document with the signatures and sat down. One of DeMille's opponents in the meeting, George Seaton, then also spoke against DeMille's removal, arguing: "The chair should appoint a committee to investigate this from top to bottom. You talk about Guild unity, gentlemen, but unless your foundation is secure, you are lost. We must take precautions so that this can never happen again. . . . I don't think that we are going to achieve it by recalling Mr DeMille." Cy Endfield endorsed a thorough investigation headed by Mankiewicz and Stevens. Endfield had attended Communist Party meetings when younger and was in the Young Communist League from 1934 to 1935. He would be named by three people when HUAC resumed hearings in 1951, and subsequently left Hollywood and America for work in the United Kingdom.[39]

Clearly seeing the prospect of DeMille resigning growing fainter by the minute, William Wyler spoke furiously:

> I am one of the twenty-five. I am also one of the fifty-five in Mr DeMille's black book. . . . I have signed other oaths too, long before any of these, and just as important. I have signed and sworn to . . . [uphold] and defend the Constitution of the United States of America against all enemies. That is what I am doing now. . . . I am sick and tired of . . . having people question my loyalty to my country. The next time I hear somebody do it, I am going to kick the Hell out of him. I don't care how old he is or how big. . . . I have seen some of these super-patriots from this room and in other rooms, and I have also seen as many real patriots, and they don't act like that or talk like that or wave the flag or pound their chests.

Wyler pointed out that DeMille had been given an opportunity to retract his ill-considered statements and flatly refused. He continued:

I was first going to say nothing. I thought enough fellows were saying things. If he had retracted it, I would still have said nothing. He didn't. He repeated it. I think he made it worse. I am one of the men that he says is accused by the State of California or by Washington. I am not. It is a lie. . . . I don't care if the Attorney General says that an organization I belong to was a Communist front. I say it is not true. . . . I have seen guys that have jobs that are conservative Republicans—good Americans—and they are scared today because they are not quite as conservative as they are asked to be by the group that is trying to run this Guild. I think that it is humiliating that everybody that has to get up has to start with proving that he is not a traitor to his country. What the Hell is this? . . . I think it is absolutely appalling. The next appalling thing I found out tonight was that I didn't know the manner in which this Board has run this Guild in the last few weeks which is absolutely staggering. . . . Well, I support this motion because there would never be any unity the way it is now with Mr Mankiewicz as President and this Board. It isn't going to work.

Wyler was applauded vehemently as he called for the Guild to be handed back over to its members rather than to be run from DeMille's office.[40]

Driving the point home, Michael Gordon stood to repeat his claims about DeMille giving information to Frank Freeman of the Producers Association, accusing DeMille of malfeasance as a board member. Seaton again defended DeMille, saying he too had spoken on a personal basis to Freeman on occasion. DeMille explained that he and Freeman were old friends and remarked: "I don't remember much detail beyond that except it was not anything divulging the Guild's affairs in any way to any detriment and in any way of the Guild." DeMille was being less than honest; he had provided detailed written reports to Freeman on SDG activities.

DeMille was now fending off attacks on several fronts. He was being criticized for speaking privately to Freeman about internal Guild affairs, for manipulating the Guild from inside his office, for corrupt practices such as deleting names from the mailing list for the recall motion, for delivering the open ballot with only one option, and for unfairly attempting to recall Mankiewicz. He balked at resigning, risking a recall motion from the entire membership and being dragged from office. Hartman had offered to withdraw his resignation demand and support Seaton's investigation. DeMille could either resign now or wait for an investigation that almost certainly would compel him to resign.[41]

John Ford Rises

With DeMille's future on the Guild's board hanging by a thread, John Ford was recognized as the next speaker. He had said nothing thus far, just sucked on his pipe during the proceedings, listening to the debate swirl around him. He had not joined the applause. Ford stood on the steps, looking away from DeMille. Eddie Salven, watching the moment from the rear, thought it showed that Ford did not want to share the stage with the embattled DeMille. After all the noise and clamor, the room went suddenly quiet in deference to the revered director as he began to speak. To identify himself to the stenographer he began, "My name is John Ford" and noted, "I am a Director of Westerns," which prompted some laughter. While his ensuing speech would become famous, mostly for its opening two sentences, Ford's talk was a rambling effort that jumped from one subject to another. He reminded the audience that he was one of the founders of the Guild. Despite claiming to be on Mankiewicz's side from the outset, Ford defended the Guild board against some of the worst accusations: "I have been sick and tired and ashamed of the whole God damn thing. I don't care which side it is. If they intend to break up the Guild, God damn it, they have pretty well done it tonight."[42]

Ford emphasized that the board itself had not demanded the recall. He was no fan of the loyalty oath and said, "Quite a few of us got up and argued vehemently and strongly and fiercely against an . . . [initiation] of a black list." The Guild had been organized to protect directors against producers, but "now, somebody wants us to throw ourselves into a news service and an intelligence service and give out to the producers what looks to me like a black list." After this strong opening, however, he tacked in another direction: "I don't know. Maybe it isn't. One side said it was and the other side said it wasn't. It looked like a black list. I protested against it. I don't know whether it passed or not." Ford argued that the Guild should not be "putting out derogatory information" as it was not the Guild's central purpose. Ford then praised Mankiewicz for doing "a great job" representing the interests of its members. He changed direction and repeated that the board of directors should not be held responsible for the recall.[43]

Having made it clear that he supported Mankiewicz and was unimpressed with DeMille's loyalty oath, Ford described DeMille as "a great guy." He said that some of the accusations against DeMille "were pretty un-American." The accusers, he felt, had "picked on probably the Dean of our profession." (The term "Dean of our profession" echoed DeMille's own publicity, which often called him the "dean of director-producers.") Ford continued: "I don't agree with C. B. DeMille. I admire him . . . I don't like him, but I admire him. Everything he said tonight he had a right to say. I don't like to hear accusations against him." Then he shifted to the crux of his argument: "If C. B. DeMille is asked to resign from this Board, somebody has achieved their purpose, the black or red. They have busted up this Guild."[44]

Ford was one of the few speakers during the entire SDG meeting who spoke emphatically in defense of DeMille. Ford concluded, however, by being even-handed about DeMille and Mankiewicz: "You know when you get the two blackest Republicans I know, Joseph Mankiewicz and C. B. DeMille and they start a fight over Communism, it is getting laughable to me. I know Joe is an ardent Republican." In his disjointed manner Ford then added that Mankiewicz had been vilified and that the Guild president deserved an apology. He reminded people that he helped give Mankiewicz a vote of confidence by the board of directors on October 18. Ford then returned to the matter of DeMille to say how he admired his fellow filmmaker's courage even if he didn't agree with him. "If Mr DeMille is recalled, your Guild is busted up," he remarked. "I just plead with you to reconsider it." Ford concluded by saying the internecine war just made "fuel for the newspaper" and calling for the meeting to adjourn. The impact of Ford's speech was immediate and inarguable; Hartman quickly withdrew his motion aimed to gain DeMille's resignation. Mankiewicz later said Ford could have swayed the meeting any way he chose. Without Ford's intervention, it seems unlikely DeMille could have survived the meeting. Even with Ford's involvement, the motion's seconder, Ralph Ceder, refused to relent and wanted to pursue DeMille's resignation, but he no longer had any support. Mankiewicz dismissed Ceder's motion.[45]

The Board Resigns

Ford may have slowed the momentum toward DeMille's immediate resignation, but his attempt to close the meeting was not successful. The directors still wanted the whole recall embarrassment to be investigated. George
Seaton continued to back an official investigation, emphasizing that "this
can never happen again." He called for a committee of five to examine the
background of the recall petition and to consider all of its ramifications.
The directors were at an impasse as to how the board might investigate its
own actions. Ford rose to his feet again and said, "I believe there is only
one alternative, and that is for the Board of Directors to resign and elect a
new Board of Directors." Having made this explosive statement, he then
backed away from his own suggestion and called on the meeting to discuss
the merits of the entire board resigning.[46]

After a lengthy debate on legal points, George Stevens made a second
speech that cut through all the rhetoric: "Having resigned once from the
Board tonight, I find myself right back in the position where I came in."
He said the investigation was necessary and worthwhile: "My only interest . . . is to see the membership investigate the situation. I stand charged.
I am not the charger." He then spoke movingly about how the Guild had
a responsibility to look out for its less successful members: "As these
founding members talked about it tonight, at one time it was for the purpose of looking out for the little fellow in this Guild. . . . Who is the man
to say I am not the little fellow, not today, perhaps not tomorrow but in a
few years. That was the purpose of this Guild when the founders started
it." Stevens's heartfelt speech had a huge impact on the audience, and his
words are still quoted today by the Directors Guild of America in its official account of the meeting. Before sitting down, however, Stevens reiterated his doubts about all that had happened: "I question this Guild, as it is
operating now. . . . I am sure that the welfare of the director—and this is
my opinion—is the secondary concern of the Board."[47]

The impact of Stevens's second speech was decisive. After some circu-
lar discussion of the legal points, one of DeMille's original supporters, Leo
McCarey, responded: "There were eleven members of the Board on the
Recall Committee. On the merits of the case, I don't want to discuss it, but
there is plenty of dissension on the Board, and it might be a great idea to
consider a whole new Board." After McCarey had finished, Ford then
moved to adopt exactly that resolution. He did so only after supporters of

both DeMille and Mankiewicz conceded the situation was untenable. Obliging the entire board to resign would save face for DeMille. It was a clever and pragmatic strategy to save DeMille's reputation and preserve the Guild's unity.[48]

The meeting began to wind down, but there were some scattered points yet to be resolved. John Farrow rose to voice his concerns about how the whole affair would be perceived by the newspaper-reading public. Addressing Mankiewicz, Farrow said, "As far as the average reader of the daily press knows an appeal went out to have you removed from office because you didn't take the loyalty oath. . . . Now they will hear the whole Board of Directors resigned. What is the conclusion of the press? What is the conclusion of the average reader of the press going to be? They are going to think that all these good, solid citizens are resigning because you and a faction won, Joe." The SDG's first president, King Vidor, warned against looking for a scapegoat as it would "do some harm to the Guild in general feelings." McCarey then reversed his earlier position, saying, "I don't want to be on record as recommending that the Board resign. It is a very serious thing. The whole idea was not to blame anybody and to leave here with unity."[49]

This time Ford stood his ground about the board resigning en masse and replied that the members could vote against the idea if they preferred. After a further exchange with McCarey he demanded that his motion go through to a vote, concluding, "The members can still vote against it, but I have been attacked enough for doing no harm, in my own mind." After further discussion, a temporary committee of five past presidents was to be selected from the six possible candidates—King Vidor, Frank Capra, John Cromwell, George Stevens, George Marshall, and Joseph L. Mankiewicz—to administer the Guild. A ballot was conducted, the motion passed unanimously, and the board resigned.[50]

Finally a committee was established to investigate the recall, with its membership to be decided by Mankiewicz. A last motion was proposed by Delmer Daves to applaud the twenty-five directors who had signed the petition, which was carried by acclamation. The meeting ended at 2:20 a.m. A small group gathered around Mankiewicz to congratulate him. One of the anti-recall signatories, Robert Parrish, felt some sadness for DeMille, but no one spoke to the director, who found himself at the center of a maelstrom of his own making as he packed his briefcase with his documents and quietly left the room alone. Even at that late hour, some celebrated their triumph in different ways. Robert Wise and a few others spent a few hours talking about the night, while George Stevens got into his car and drove for miles in a jubilant mood.[51]

4

The Aftermath

In the last few minutes of the October 22, 1950, general meeting of the Screen Directors Guild, Mabel Walker Willebrandt resigned from her position as legal counsel. She had been a staunch supporter of Cecil B. DeMille and his anti-Communist drive, later comparing him to Abraham Lincoln for his stand. Joseph Mankiewicz declined her resignation, and Willebrandt, resuming her active role, advised that the proposed interim structure of five past presidents was unlawful. In response Joseph Mankiewicz, John Ford, Frank Capra, George Stevens, George Sidney, and others formed an interim SDG board. Ford was first vice president, Capra was second vice president, Stevens was secretary, and Sidney was treasurer. Others appointed to the temporary board were Claude Binyon, Delmer Daves, John Farrow, Henry Hathaway, Walter Lang, H. C. Potter, Mark Robson, George Seaton, Charles Vidor, William Wellman, and Fred Zinnemann. The new interim board featured a strong contingent of those who acted against the recall. Most of DeMille's conservative stalwarts were passed over. Even so, the first initiative to emerge from the new administration was the adoption of the loyalty oath at the first interim board meeting on October 25, 1950. None of this would have been surprising for those who attended the October 22 meeting. Mankiewicz had said earlier that few members opposed the oath, but they "resented the compulsory aspect of it, their lack of an opportunity to discuss it and the open signed ballot." However, the oath was voluntary for only a short time. In 1951 the Guild changed its constitution and by-laws to require new members to sign an oath, and the rule was ratified by the membership on May 27. Mankiewicz left Hollywood soon afterward, having declined to serve a second term as president—even though DeMille, as he had promised earlier, was prepared to nominate him.[1]

Mankiewicz's attitude toward the oath was complex. He could see no point in any loyalty oath that went beyond the legal guidelines of the Taft–Hartley Act, which compelled union leaders to sign the oath. Repeatedly, at different SDG board discussions, Mankiewicz refused to discuss the loyalty oath, insisting it was a dead issue. When directly questioned about the oath at the October 22 meeting, he said, "Please never when you refer to any opinion of mine concerning the mandatory loyalty oath of this Guild, leave out the word 'mandatory.' I have never implied in any way an opposition to a loyalty oath. . . . I did not want anyone to infer from what I said that this Guild would have defeated the mandatory loyalty oath. I still say that I do not think and I cannot be made to think that the result of any election on an open ballot is an honest reflection of the people participating in that election." The open ballot—which identified the name of the member and which way they voted—was one of the catalysts for the general meeting on October 22, 1950. Mankiewicz's position was restated after the meeting, on October 26, 1950, when he issued an open letter to members in an advertisement to the trade papers claiming that he had never opposed a loyalty oath. He called on SDG members to sign a voluntary version.[2]

This attempt to calm the waters just caused further ructions. His advertisement certainly overstated matters, as the loyalty oath and the blacklist, to which it was linked, were mentioned before and during the October 22, 1950, meeting. Many of his fellow directors believed Mankiewicz strongly opposed the loyalty oath. Reacting to Mankiewicz's advertisement, Frank Capra resigned from the board for a second time, writing in a letter to the board members, "A calm and dispassionate reading of the minutes of the last three board meetings will certainly show that Mr Mankiewicz was in *violent opposition* to a loyalty oath for all Guild members. He repeatedly made the statement that he would never sign one as a member." He continued: "Mr Mankiewicz's letter to the members is not to me a sincere attempt to heal the rift. It is the vindication and sanctification for himself and his disciples, and consignment to hell for the opposition. His idea of meeting you half way is to pay for half the expenses of your funeral." Looking back at the period, the director Howard W. Koch thought Mankiewicz was going to break the Guild.[3]

Other directors including Andrew Stone wanted to print an announcement in trade papers refuting the October 26, 1950, advertisement, while Al Rogell told other DeMille supporters that Mankiewicz should not be allowed to get away with "this falsification." Aside from Capra, Mankiewicz's opponents took no action. Mankiewicz's supporters were divided as well. For Christmas that year Mankiewicz sent a copy of the petition to all his twenty-five partisans. Richard Brooks would frame his copy, and Robert Parrish would keep his and later publish both a facsimile and the text in his autobiography. Joseph Losey, who was blacklisted in 1951, was not happy to be on Mankiewicz's list and thought the subsequent adoption of a loyalty oath was tantamount to a betrayal.[4]

Mankiewicz saw the October 22, 1950, meeting as a personal and professional watershed. Two bound copies of the meeting's transcript were made. Mankiewicz was presented with one as president; the second was kept in the SDG archives. Over the years, Mankiewicz would study his copy closely, writing comments on almost every page and underlining key passages from everyone's speeches. The record would prove useful. A few years after the meeting, Mankiewicz wrote to MGM studio executive Nicholas Schenck to clarify political issues in order to clear his own return to Hollywood. He restated his position: he had signed the Taft–Hartley loyalty oath several times as president of the SDG, but he did not consider the Guild a properly constituted authority to enforce a mandatory oath. Mankiewicz confirmed that he did not publicly protest against the oath. Yet in his copy of the transcript, Mankiewicz noted in the margins that he had opposed the loyalty oath. It is a confusion that exists to this day. Many continue to believe that the meeting challenged the validity of the loyalty oath. Some film historians have described Mankiewicz's subsequent actions in introducing the oath as a bewildering retreat. Yet explaining the so-called reversal is simple: there wasn't one. A voluntary oath is entirely consistent with the position Mankiewicz had taken repeatedly at the board, as well as during the SDG meetings. While the issue of the oath triggered events that led to the meeting, the loyalty oath was really only one factor in the upheaval. Even in its mandatory form, the loyalty oath was supported by the vast majority of the SDG members before, during, and after the meeting.[5]

If the loyalty oath was not the central issue, the way DeMille and his anti-Communist allies conducted themselves provided some of the fuel for the revolt. DeMille's actions in stacking meetings and shutting down debate after his election to the board in December 1947 had infuriated many directors. Some SDG members sought political and personal payback for DeMille's aggressive style over the previous two years, beginning with his group's bid to control the SDG board. Speaking at the October 22,

1950, meeting, John Cromwell reminded the group of the role DeMille's ally Sam Wood had played in testifying to HUAC in 1947, when Cromwell was named as a fellow traveler. He expressed his pride in the SDG board's forthright defense of himself in 1947. Cromwell went on to speak about his subsequent horror in seeing Wood elected to the board just a few months later, with DeMille's support. It seemed that DeMille just rubbed people the wrong way. Edward Dmytryk, who was in jail for contempt of Congress at the time of the October 22, 1950, meeting, later wrote that he was not a fan of revenge but would have enjoyed seeing DeMille deposed. For Dmytryk, DeMille was a hard man to like, but easy to loathe.[6]

Certainly, many liberals in the organization relished DeMille's resignation, but as John Huston later told the FBI, the central reason for DeMille's removal was the "highly undemocratic" manner in which the leader of the conservatives had attempted to recall Mankiewicz. When the facts were revealed, he "was compelled to resign." Over the course of a few weeks, DeMille had alienated most sections of the directorial community, and George Stevens's eloquent attack of the recall represented his final defeat.[7]

The Guild's use of the open and signed ballot was discarded before the October 22, 1950, meeting. It is unlikely that the blacklist provision would have survived, given the clear and stated opposition of both Mankiewicz and Ford. Mankiewicz would later say that he stayed in office for the remaining six months of his term and, with the help of the new board of directors, developed a revised constitution and by-laws to prevent a recurrence of the attempted recall and de facto blacklisting. It is uncertain precisely what changes actually occurred. It is clear, however, that Mabel Walker Willebrandt, as the Guild's legal counsel, continued her aggressive attack on the Radio and Television Directors Guild, which included branding her opponents "Communists" at every opportunity. The Guild neither backed away from the mandatory loyalty oath nor ushered in a stronger anti-HUAC administration. The SDG in fact continued to work with the Motion Picture Industry Council, which supported HUAC's 1951 investigation, arguing that all guilds should support "any legally constituted body that has as its objective exposure and destruction of the international Communist conspiracy." Moreover, after Herbert Biberman returned from serving his prison sentence for contempt of Congress in 1952, the Guild refused to readmit him as a member despite the fact that he was one of its founders. Vincent Sherman also found little official support from the Guild when he was graylisted and could not find work in 1953.[8]

In more general terms the Guild did return its focus to directors' professional business. As a direct result of the October 22, 1950, meeting, Joseph Youngerman was appointed executive secretary, which proved to be an inspired move. Supported by John Farrow, William Wellman, and George Sidney, Youngerman was seen as a person who could get different groups to work together. His appointment was a critical move as the Guild not only had suffered political schisms; it was almost broke. In a short time, however, Youngerman had restored the Guild's finances to the point where it was able to develop a new building on Sunset Boulevard in Los Angeles. Youngerman's dedication was outstanding. He even sold his house to move to an apartment closer to the SDG's office. He also repaired relations with the RTDG. Within ten years Youngerman had helped arrange an important merger with the New York–based RTDG to form the Directors Guild of America (DGA). He also brought in directors from Florida, Chicago, and San Francisco. Many people, such as the new president, George Sidney, saw him as a pivotal figure in the reinvigoration of the Guild with the creation of an effective pension plan and residuals and awards dinners. The appointment of Youngerman with his professional and diligent approach helped lay the groundwork for today's modern Guild with its thousands of members.[9]

DeMille was ostracized for a short time by the Hollywood directorial community, and his friends and associates say he was personally crushed by the October 22, 1950, meeting. According to his publicity assistant, Phil Koury, DeMille acted despondently at lunch the next day, barely eating and muttering that the country was in deep trouble. The director told the actor Henry Wilcoxon, a close professional colleague, that it was one of the worst events of his life. DeMille wrote to one of his allies, Clarence Brown: "The 'boys' are now in complete control. Attack upon Board and me led by Huston, Hartman, Wyler, Cromwell, Stevens, Potter et cetera. Regrets and regards."[10]

It took DeMille almost a month to make his formal report on the meeting to the FBI. Others were quicker off the mark. Informant T-22, as he was known, reported almost immediately that the board had been asked to resign because of controversy over the loyalty oath. Another informant, T-23, believed the SDG meeting could "destroy any united action on the part of the Motion Picture Industry Council in regard to the adoption of an industry loyalty oath program." T-14 reported that a number of the people "supporting Mankiewicz were communist sympathisers."

A later report to J. Edgar Hoover stated that DeMille had been asked for "information concerning the controversy which took place in the Screen Directors Guild over the installation of a loyalty oath." It noted that as an "Executive Board Member, [he] was able to furnish complete information" about people who opposed the oath along with "tactics employed by them." Even so, DeMille's belated version of events did not cast Mankiewicz in a negative light. Despite his removal from the board, DeMille did not stop supplying information to the FBI. As late as 1954 an FBI memorandum noted that DeMille "can furnish complete confidential information concerning the personnel and policies of the Screen Directors Guild."[11]

DeMille still had his supporters, and he had a friend in John Ford. Ford sent a letter to his fellow director following the October 22, 1950, meeting in which he stated, "I wish to have it formally recorded on paper, with my signature attached that from the so-called membership meeting of the Screen Directors' of America, Sunday evening October 22, 1950, you emerged as a very great gentleman." Ford then phoned DeMille a few days after the meeting to say that "Sunday night was a disgusting thing to see" and that the directors were "not a wolf pack, but a mice pack attacking you." He praised DeMille in the phone call as "a magnificent figure so far above that goddamn pack of rats. . . . I have recommended men for courage in battle, but I have never seen courage as you displayed Sunday night. God bless you, you're a great man." He concluded by saying he had spoken to many people in Hollywood, including Mankiewicz, who all agreed that DeMille would emerge from the meeting "greater than ever."[12]

Perhaps Ford's main concern was to smooth over the unseemly divisions within the Guild and to ensure that DeMille would remain active in it. He was especially keen to calm any tensions between DeMille and Mankiewicz. The letter and phone call also demonstrate that Ford and DeMille came from the same era—perhaps a more gentlemanly and respectful time—when once an issue was dealt with, it was time to shake hands and move on. His long-time associate Dick L'Estrange, whom DeMille had mentioned in his speech at the meeting, also sent a note expressing his regret. Both directors got the same response: "Thank you for your friendly expression, attack I am used to, kindness moves me very deeply." In contrast, Willebrandt, who compared DeMille to Abraham Lincoln, received a glowing reply saying that DeMille would cherish her letter for the rest of his life. In any case, DeMille's professional reputation was not immediately affected. In 1952 he was awarded the Irving G. Thalberg

Memorial Award, and his film *The Greatest Show on Earth* (1952) won the Academy Award for best picture.[13]

Meanwhile, steps were taken to resolve the lingering differences inside the Guild. After the October 22, 1950, meeting, DeMille stopped attending regular meetings and played no real role in Guild operations, but some tried to bring him back into the fold. Executive Secretary Youngerman, President Sidney, and almost certainly Ford were involved in such attempts. At the Screen Directors Guild Awards in 1953, DeMille earned a standing ovation when he received the first ever D. W. Griffith Lifetime Achievement Award. As DeMille had had only one film nominated for the Guild awards since 1938, it seems clear that this award was a peace offering. DeMille had always admired D. W. Griffith and would later write about him reverently in his autobiography as "a great genius." Before the loyalty oath issue exploded, DeMille had helped organize a D. W. Griffith Memorial for the SDG. Sidney, who had been a marginal ally of DeMille's at the meeting, introduced the award ceremony. However, Youngerman, who had been a prop man for DeMille at the start of his career, also played a role in instituting the award and choosing its first recipient—a conciliatory gesture. No direct evidence exists that Ford was involved in the award, but there are enough indications to suggest he may have had a role. After all, Ford and DeMille were two of only six people who paid their respects to D. W. Griffith at the funeral home on July 26, 1948. Ford, who would be an obvious choice to be the first recipient, won the award the following year.[14]

At the 1953 SDG Awards ceremony, many of the same directors who had attacked DeMille in 1950 stood and applauded him. Yet some were not willing to forgive. The table at which Fred Zinnemann sat did not join the ovation when DeMille was presented with the award. Some of his opponents, such as Mankiewicz and Zinnemann, would hold on to bitter memories. While DeMille still made public speeches with references to Communism and reported to the FBI, he shifted away from the internal politics of the SDG and spent most of his energy on filmmaking. He entered into a financially successful period of his film career, with the highly successful *The Greatest Show on Earth* and the remake of *The Ten Commandments* (1956), which became one of the highest grossing films of the 1950s. He remained a venerated figure in Hollywood.[15]

The loyalty oath was part of the DGA constitution for the next sixteen years. It was so entrenched in the DGA that it took a U.S. Supreme Court decision in 1966 to finally dislodge it. The issue came to a head in 1965 when the DGA wanted to amalgamate with the Screen Directors International Guild, which did not ask its members to take such an oath. The International Guild mostly represented documentary filmmakers on the East Coast and had a stronger left-wing culture than the conservative DGA. For the amalgamation to progress, the DGA insisted that all members sign the oath. Six International Guild members—Leo Hurwitz, Lee R. Bobker, Robert Braverman, Gene Searchinger, Darrell Random, and Hilary T. Harris—refused to do so and were denied membership. In response to the legal challenge from these six members, President Sidney argued that the Guild had prospered with the loyalty oath in place. The DGA insisted that no director had ever been turned down for membership for refusing to sign the oath. Despite the assurances, Robert Braverman found that he was ineligible for membership in the newly merged organization for failing to sign the oath. After being rejected by the District Court, the six directors appealed, and the Court of Appeals found the DGA's oath was "offensive to non-communist labor leaders."[16]

The ruling criticized that the vague nature of the oath was a potential weapon to punish people who differed politically from the union's majority or who challenged the union's leadership. The court believed that the use of broad language in the oath restricted the political activities of those "who [would] sign it conscientiously" and said it discouraged people from joining political groups and from espousing controversial political positions: "All but the hardiest may well hesitate to join organizations if they know that by such a proscription they will be permanently disqualified from public employment." The court also attacked the "vague portions of the DGA oath" that unreasonably limited the political freedom of the union's membership. There was "no justifiable interest in regulating the political beliefs of its membership, at least where those beliefs have not been translated into conduct that is inimical to the union's interests." The court concluded: "Under these circumstances, we think that this oath goes beyond what the union's interests reasonably require, that its enforcement serves to deter the political activity of the union members, and that failure to sign it is an insufficient indication of Communist beliefs to warrant expulsion from the union." In response, the DGA unsuccessfully appealed to the U.S. Supreme Court. Only then, when all legal avenues were exhausted, did the DGA discontinue the oath.[17]

The court's decision not only indirectly criticized DeMille and Willebrandt, the originators of the oath; it also drew attention to the administrations headed by Joseph Mankiewicz, George Sidney, Robert Wise, and Frank Capra, who had cemented the oath in SDG practices. In a later interview Mankiewicz said the court decision vindicated his position, but that is hardly a credible argument. Even if Mankiewicz had only supported a voluntary oath, as he often insisted, the distinction between his position and DeMille's was razor thin. Since he himself backed a compulsory version in 1951, there remains only the significant difference over the blacklist provision between the two men.[18]

For the most part, the SDG meeting and its loyalty oath controversy were forgotten for a long time. The first account of the meeting came from DeMille's publicity assistant, Phil Koury, in 1959—almost a decade after the event. In his memoir, Koury called it a minor row that happened periodically in a highly strung industry. The conservative Koury saw the issue as an attempt by the board to put to rest rumors that the Guild contained Communists. He gave the meeting only frivolous treatment, saying that during the long meeting DeMille was the only director who did not go to the bathroom, prompting a journalist to quip that he must have the strongest bladder in Hollywood. Certainly, Koury did not see the meeting as significant. However, interpretations of the meeting were to become distorted and misrepresented by participants, biographers, and historians over the next five decades, and the underlying causes would become twisted and almost unrecognizable. The images of Ford, DeMille, and Mankiewicz would also be affected. The meeting was over, but now the myth-making began.[19]

Before the storm, Cecil B. DeMille, Gloria Swanson, and Billy Wilder enjoyed working together on *Sunset Boulevard* (1950), which was released just before the October 22 SDG meeting. Wilder would become a strident opponent of DeMille over his treatment of Mankiewicz. (Photofest)

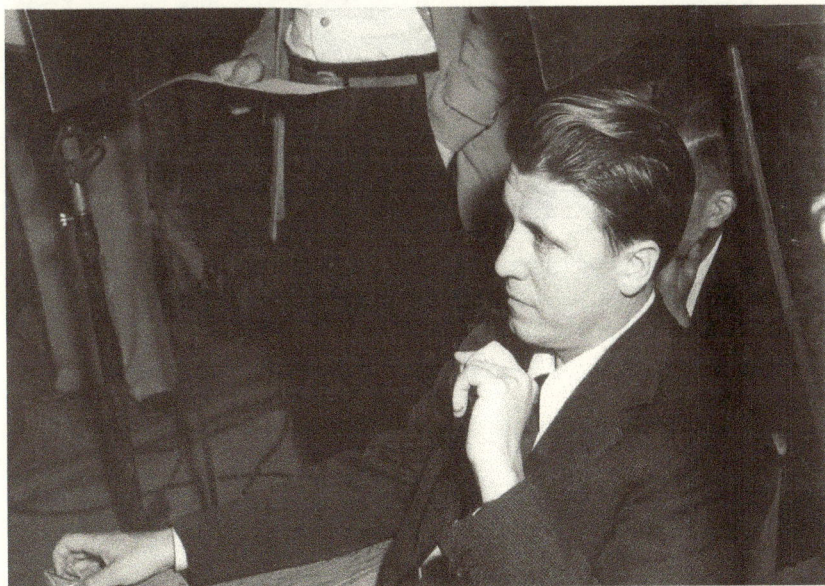

George Stevens would play a key role in ensuring that DeMille was removed from the SDG board for his actions in recalling Mankiewicz. (Columbia / The Kobal Collection / Lippman, Irving)

Frank Capra in the production of his *Why We Fight* films in 1945. Capra would initially back DeMille, but he resigned in protest about the behavior of the De-Mille camp. He resigned again after the October 22, 1950, SDG meeting, object-ing to the manner in which Mankiewicz publicized the voluntary oath. (Photofest)

John Ford (*center*) on the set of *Rio Grande* (1950), which he was completing at the time of the SDG meeting. Ford played a conciliatory role throughout the meeting and beyond in an attempt to end the dispute without public division. (Photofest)

William Wyler (*left*) and the dramatist and screenwriter Terence Rattigan (*center*) making a documentary during the Second World War. Wyler would refer to his war record in his strong speech attacking DeMille, and at one point he threatened to kick him. (Photofest)

Sam Wood (*center*) looking at a model designed by William Cameron Menzies (*right*) for *Pride of the Yankees* (1943). Cecil B. DeMille and Wood would go on to wrest control from the liberal leadership of the SDG in 1947. (Photofest)

(*Left to right*) Rouben Mamoulian, William Wyler, Mervyn LeRoy, Billy Wilder, and Lewis Milestone in the 1940s. Mamoulian's remarks about his accent at the SDG meeting would be used in a far more sinister way as the years progressed. (Photofest)

Al Rogell (*right*) on the set of *Private Affairs* (1940). Rogell would work loyally for DeMille throughout this controversial period. He would defend DeMille's role in the 1980s. (Photofest)

John Huston in 1950. Huston was the first person to sign the petition to defend Mankiewicz. Part of his short speech at the SDG meeting would be quoted by directors for decades. (Photofest)

Don Hartman directing *It Had to Be You* (1947). Hartman would demand that DeMille resign from the SDG board for his actions in recalling Mankiewicz. (Photofest)

Richard Brooks in later years. Brooks, as a young director, signed the petition for Mankiewicz and considered making a film about the meeting in the 1980s. (Douglass K. Daniel)

Joseph Mankiewicz dominated Hollywood with his writing and directing before becoming the center of the dispute that gripped the SDG during 1950. (L. Tom Perry Special Collections, Harold B. Lee Library, Brigham Young University, Provo, Utah)

Cecil B. DeMille was at the height of his cinematic powers in 1950. DeMille had one of the most successful movies of the year with *Samson and Delilah,* which was released in late 1949, and dominated the SDG. (L. Tom Perry Special Collections, Harold B. Lee Library, Brigham Young University, Provo, Utah)

5

Mankiewicz and the Making of the Myth

During the October 22, 1950, Screen Directors Guild meeting, John Ford described both Cecil B. DeMille and Joseph Mankiewicz as the "blackest Republicans" he knew, and said that when "they start a fight over communism, it is getting laughable to me. I know Joe is an ardent Republican." In the 1950s being a "black Republican" meant harboring a deep ideological commitment to conservatism, to the point of being a reactionary. Mankiewicz responded by describing himself as a "Pennsylvanian Republican." Yet when Mankiewicz came to read the transcript in later years, he crossed out the word "Republican" and wrote in red pen "Democrat." Mankiewicz had redefined his political past, and many historians and biographers have fallen into step.[1]

After the meeting Mankiewicz made stronger liberal statements. He inserted a scene into his next film, *People Will Talk* (1951), as his biographer Kenneth L. Geist has pointed out, that mirrored the conclusion of the night. At the end of the meeting DeMille had packed his briefcase with his files and then abjectly left the room. A scene in *People Will Talk* depicts an inquiry in which the vanquished Doctor Rodney Elwell (Hume Cronyn), a McCarthyite figure who attempts to destroy the reputations of opponents by digging into their pasts, walks away in a similar fashion. Mankiewicz's adaptation of *Julius Caesar* (1953) can also be read as political commentary on the Cold War and McCarthyism. His liberal tolerance had clear limits, however, particularly when it came to Communism. This would become obvious with *The Quiet American* (1958). The Graham Greene novel on which the film was based had created a furor over its depiction of the assassination of a naive American who foolishly enters the conflict between the Viet Minh and the French. Published in 1955, the novel was prophetic about the future U.S. participation in the Vietnam War. It took a bitter view of American involvement in the Far East, predating the polarizing anti–Vietnam War protests by more than a decade. In Mankiewicz's adaptation the CIA agent Alden Pyle—called "the American" in the film version—became an innocent victim of the British. Many commentators believe that Mankiewicz had been influenced by an anti-Communist lobby group, the American Friends of Vietnam, to reverse the book's anti-American perspective. Indeed, copies of the script were later found in the group's papers. Mankiewicz insisted, however, that he had not been pressured to change the story.[2]

After the harsh critical reaction to *The Quiet American*, Mankiewicz moved as far away from politics as he could with his next film, *Suddenly, Last Summer* (1959), based on the Tennessee Williams play. The film gained more notoriety than acclaim for its veiled depiction of homosexuality. It would be three years before Mankiewicz returned to the job of directing, when he accepted the challenge of rescuing *Cleopatra* in 1962. At some level he must have compared himself with DeMille, who had crafted an earlier treatment of the same subject in 1934. He was not the only director to take on the challenge of a DeMille-style epic, and other directors had been successful. After the box office strength of DeMille's *Samson and Delilah* (1949), a cycle of successful epic films began: Mervyn LeRoy's *Quo Vadis* (1951), William Dieterle's *Salome* (1953), Henry Koster's *The Robe* (1953), Michael Curtiz's *The Egyptian* (1954), and Howard Hawks's *Land of the Pharaohs* (1955). Of course, DeMille would then surpass them all in 1956 with his final film, *The Ten Commandments*. After the release of DeMille's film, William Wyler had nervously taken on the challenge of making what he called a Cecil B. DeMille–style film when he directed *Ben-Hur* in 1959. By then, Mankiewicz and DeMille's conflict had long since been forgotten by all but a few industry insiders. Nonetheless, *Cleopatra* offered Mankiewicz an opportunity to trump DeMille in the epic style and to outdo his former political rival. Mankiewicz would have been less than human not to have seen the ironic possibility of beating his old foe at his own game.

Even though the film eventually proved a success at the box office, the project had threatened to be a debacle from the beginning of production. Rouben Mamoulian left the helm when spending spiraled out of control. The studio insisted that shooting resume, even with the script half-finished. As a result, for many months Mankiewicz directed by day and wrote at night. At the end of a physically draining schedule, he decided it would be best to offer it as two separate films. The producer, Darryl F. Zanuck, however, had other ideas. He fired Mankiewicz and edited the length down from seven hours of footage to four, then to a final cut of three hours, which was released in 1963. Mankiewicz later claimed that the film's value had been lost. Despite the problems, the film attracted some good reviews, including from Bosley Crowther of the *New York Times.* However, most reviewers were less favorable, with Judith Crist in the *New York Herald Tribune* famously labeling the film a "Monumental Mouse." The film topped the box office for the year, but with the amount spent on its production, it was considered a disaster that nearly bankrupted Twentieth Century Fox. Mankiewicz deleted it from his filmography and refused to discuss it with interviewers. He followed *Cleopatra* with an attempt at a comeback film, *The Honey Pot* (1967), which was a commercial failure. It would be Mankiewicz's last screenplay. He directed *There Was a Crooked Man . . .* in 1970, but this was not successful either, although it gained some good reviews. His career was partially redeemed with the release of *Sleuth* in 1972, which enjoyed positive critical reviews and an Academy Award nomination for best director. Yet even this relative success did not encourage Mankiewicz; he never directed or wrote another film.[3]

In more general terms Mankiewicz was not in critical favor in the 1960s. Andrew Sarris placed directors in a hierarchy in his highly influential book *The American Cinema* (1968). The book introduced the United States to the auteur theory, with the director as the key driving force of a film. Of the central participants in the SDG meeting, only John Ford made the pantheon—the highest level. DeMille was placed in the second rank, and Mankiewicz was classed as a "fallen idol" and placed in the fifth. Sarris described Mankiewicz's cinema as "intelligence without inspiration" and his technique as "pedestrian."[4]

It was during these years of directorial inactivity that Mankiewicz began to talk about the meeting and to give his own version of events. The idea that Ford attacked DeMille at the SDG meeting emerged when Mankiewicz was interviewed by Peter Bogdanovich in 1967. Mankiewicz said he opposed the oath. He spoke about returning to Hollywood from Europe and being confronted with the dispute. Items began to appear in the media describing him as a Communist, he said, which threatened the end of his directorial career. Mankiewicz described the October 22, 1950, meeting as running for four hours, with the DeMille group holding its ground. He said he sat there wondering which side Ford would support, as he was a major figure in the Guild and could sway the meeting if he spoke up. According to Mankiewicz, after DeMille had finished his speech, Ford raised his hand and identified himself to the stenographer with the words: "My name's John Ford. I make Westerns." Mankiewicz described how Ford applauded DeMille's films and his work as a director. Changing tone, staring straight at DeMille, Ford said that he did not like him, or what he had been saying. Ford moved for a vote of confidence in Mankiewicz, and the meeting abruptly ended. By rolling Ford's several speeches into one, Mankiewicz recast the director's involvement to make it seem that DeMille bore the brunt of Ford's verbal attack and that it was this speech that curtailed the meeting. In this short interview, the perception of John Ford's role at the SDG meeting began to change to that of a more heroic intervention.[5]

Mankiewicz again highlighted the SDG meeting when he returned to Hollywood in 1975 to celebrate Joseph Youngerman's twenty-five years of service as SDG executive secretary. Mankiewicz wanted to let a new generation know about Ford and the loyalty oath. He felt he "was boring them; boring the bejesus out of them" with his memories of the event, and indeed, the audience began talking during his speech. One member of the audience, the director Robert Wise, recalled that Mankiewicz spent too much time talking about the SDG meeting when people really were waiting to hear from Youngerman. When Mankiewicz had finished, the master of ceremonies, Carl Reiner, joked that Mankiewicz's speech had the same problem as *Cleopatra*—it went on for too long. Mankiewicz would be sure to enliven his future accounts of the meeting.[6]

Robert Parrish, a member of the group of petitioners who supported Mankiewicz, also gave a version of events in his memoirs—soon after the Youngerman occasion. Parrish idolized Ford, seeing him as a great director and as a mentor figure. In the early part of his career, Parrish had sought guidance from Ford on how to be a director and had worked with him as an assistant on films such as *Stagecoach* (1939) and *The Long Voyage Home* (1940). Ford served as his commanding officer in the Office of Strategic Services during the Second World War. Writing his account, Parrish relied on his memory, a copy of the petition, and an article from *Variety* of October 24, 1950. Mankiewicz made extensive comments on one of the drafts for Parrish's book.[7]

Since Mankiewicz was the sole owner of a copy of the SDG meeting transcript, outside of the Directors Guild of America archives, it is remarkable that he did not correct a whole series of errors in Parrish's account. Some of Parrish's faults are minor and can be attributed to the difficulty of recalling a meeting held more than twenty-five years previously. Parrish confused Fritz Lang with Rouben Mamoulian in retelling the anecdote about being embarrassed about his accent. Repeating an error in the *Variety* article, he wrote that George Marshall stayed silent for the whole meeting; Marshall did in fact speak, albeit just once and only briefly. Following editorial advice from Mankiewicz, Parrish misquoted William Wyler as saying he was going to punch DeMille in the nose; Wyler actually said that he was going to kick DeMille. A young director was cited as saying that he had learned everything from DeMille but was now ashamed of their mentor–protégé relationship, but no such comment is in the transcript.

In Parrish's account, Ford is quoted as saying to DeMille that he did not like him or what he had been saying at the meeting. Parrish then adds that DeMille stared straight ahead for thirty seconds, after which Ford called for the board to resign. Most serious of all, DeMille is accused of saying that some of his opponents were "foreign born." Delmer Daves is depicted as criticizing DeMille for his attack on these directors and then breaking down. In a later interview with the film historian Barry Norman, Parrish amended his story to say that Mamoulian rose to complain about DeMille's linking of the signatories to their foreign origins. According to Parrish, Mamoulian demanded that DeMille withdraw the comment and felt fear of his own background for the first time.[8]

In political terms, Parrish connected DeMille's drive to recall Mankiewicz to the Red hunting of both Senator Joseph McCarthy and Richard Nixon. Mankiewicz told Parrish that what he called the "Cecil B. DeMille Foundation for Americanism" was the central source for the Tenney Committee, which then passed files and information along to HUAC and McCarthy. Mankiewicz warned Parrish that the foundation had a dossier on him. Parrish wrote his book in the post-Nixon era and looked back at the SDG meeting and DeMille's role in it through that prism. From 1972 to 1974 the United States had been preoccupied by the Watergate scandal, which led to the impeachment process of President Nixon, eventually forcing his resignation. The rhetoric concerning the meeting—dealing with governance and corruption—is close to the issues surrounding the Watergate break-in and its later cover-up. To strengthen the connection,

Nixon had been a member of HUAC when it investigated Hollywood in 1947. Indeed, his work on the committee had bolstered his prominence and helped open the door to his vice presidency under President Dwight D. Eisenhower. Other writers would follow Parrish's example and tie DeMille to Nixon. The author Greg Mitchell later wrote the story of the October 22, 1950, meeting as a counterpoint to Nixon's vicious electoral campaign against Helen Gahagan Douglas.[9]

Embracing the Nixon theme, Mankiewicz began to toy with writing his own recollections of the meeting, called "Cecil B. DeMille's Impeachment of Me as President." Unsuccessfully presenting the idea to Tom Guinzburg, publisher at the Viking Press, Mankiewicz said that DeMille's ultimate aim was the control of every member of every union in the United States through a mandatory oath. Mankiewicz believed that the "DeMille Foundation for Americanism" was run by Tom Girdler of Republic Steel, notorious for his violent strikebreaking in the 1930s. It is uncertain where Mankiewicz picked up this idea, as Girdler is mentioned only marginally in the DeMille archives. Girdler gave a $500 donation to DeMille's foundation in 1945 and DeMille thanked him for his "generous help" in 1955. He was an occasional correspondent over the years but appears to have played no formal role. Mankiewicz later tried to get a draft of his own account published by *American Film* magazine, which rejected it, citing a lack of space. As late as 1987 he still claimed to be writing the book centering on the SDG meeting.[10]

After being rejected by book and magazine publishers, Mankiewicz supplied similar details, as well as the SDG meeting transcript, to Kenneth Geist, who used it in his biography of Mankiewicz, *Pictures Will Talk,* published in 1978. Geist believed that Mankiewicz's status as "the thinking man's Hollywood director" of the 1950s had been downgraded by Andrew Sarris. While he admired his cinema and repeated some of his claims, Geist did not present an entirely laudatory version of Mankiewicz's role at the SDG meeting: he included how Mankiewicz introduced the voluntary loyalty oath but concluded that his justifications were inconsistent. Geist's biography also differs from earlier accounts. He did quote the key line from the transcript from Ford: "I don't agree with C. B. DeMille. I admire him . . . I don't like him, but I admire him. . . . If Mr DeMille is recalled, your Guild is busted up." However, he showed Ford was important but that other directors, such as George Stevens and William Wyler, also played a significant part in defeating DeMille. In fact, it was a collective blast of anger that destroyed DeMille.

In general terms, the Mankiewicz biography helped revive interest in the former SDG president's cinema. Mankiewicz was celebrated in France, with two film festivals assessing his work in 1980 and 1981 and his career highlighted in *Cahiers du Cinéma* in October 1980. A Mankiewicz retrospective followed at the Museum of Modern Art in 1981, where Sidney Poitier credited Mankiewicz with giving him the break he needed, proclaiming him a "liberal" and "a revolutionary." Festivals would follow in London in 1982, Germany in 1983, Holland in 1984, and Madrid in 1985.[11]

Parrish's book and Geist's biography had opened fresh windows onto the SDG meeting, and so did the documentary on DeMille produced by Barry Norman for the BBC in 1981, on the centenary of DeMille's birth. Norman argued that Mankiewicz was a true liberal and DeMille wanted him removed from the presidency because of his left-wing views. About this time, Mankiewicz became far more caustic about DeMille and was also more determined to call himself a liberal.[12]

Mankiewicz added elements to his account in the following years. His interview with Michel Ciment in 1983, published only in French, has rarely been referenced. In this pivotal interview, Mankiewicz redefined his own political stance. He said he had never joined any Popular Front groups such as the Hollywood Anti-Nazi League in the 1930s. His brother Herman was the conservative, he said, while he was a liberal who supported Franklin D. Roosevelt. He admitted introducing the loyalty oath after the meeting but said he believed it would eventually be deemed anticonstitutional. He claimed to have predicted the inevitability of the 1966 Supreme Court decision that did just that. His reasoning is difficult to follow, but he argued that the loyalty oath was needed to end the infighting in the Guild and allow people to go back to work. If he had not introduced it, the Guild would have been destroyed. Mankiewicz also began to highlight his opponent's alleged anti-Semitism, telling Ciment that DeMille had written his autobiography without ever mentioning the name of his mother because she was Jewish. At the October 22, 1950, meeting, Mankiewicz claimed, DeMille used an anti-Semitic accent when he pronounced foreign-sounding names: Wilder became "Vilder" and Zinnemann, "Tzinnemann."[13]

This new facet of Mankiewicz's revised account had been circulating in directorial circles for many years—even decades. Billy Wilder had spoken about it in an interview with Geist on October 11, 1972. Fred Zinnemann repeated the claims in an interview with George Stevens Jr. in

1982 during the making of a documentary about his father, *George Stevens: A Filmmaker's Journey* (1984). Zinnemann said DeMille decided that Mankiewicz "was not worthy to be president" and began "a campaign of intimidation to have him removed." During the SDG meeting, Zinnemann recounts, DeMille mispronounced names while delivering his speech, to accentuate their foreign origins or their Jewish ancestry. However, the full transcript of the interview suggests a different picture. Zinnemann was filming in Europe at the time of the SDG meeting and only heard about the story secondhand. Stevens Jr. asked him whether DeMille made life difficult for directors from overseas. Zinnemann replied, "I think Joe Mankiewicz can probably tell you dramatically what happened. But I remember that *Mr DeMille stood up and said, 'Mr Vyler, Mr Vilder, Mr Tzinnemann.' And he made a point in pronouncing it in that way to accentuate the fact that we weren't born in this country.*" The documentary includes only the text in italics, but in context it is clear that Zinnemann was repeating a story about the meeting told to him by Mankiewicz. He made no secret that he was not present at the SDG meeting in this or later interviews.[14]

Before the documentary was produced, Mankiewicz had written a letter to George Stevens Jr. praising his father's role in the SDG meeting. The letter contains a savage attack on DeMille, comparing him to McCarthy and even the Gestapo. Stevens Jr. turned to Mankiewicz as a key interviewee for the subsequent documentary. In an initial interview with the researcher Susan Winslow in 1981, Mankiewicz retold his story about the accents. He then repeated the account for the filming: "*DeMille spoke, I spoke and the usual speeches were made and DeMille started right off . . . , in an attempt to show the foreign influences that were at work.* He read off the 25 names of the men who had secured the injunction of my recall. And he says, this one example, and I give a fair imitation of him . . . [Villiam] Wyler, Fred [Ts]innemann, Billy [V]ilder, and the connotations are [un]mistakable." Mankiewicz then painted DeMille as being booed by the assembled directors. When editing the documentary, Stevens Jr. used the initial part of Mankiewicz's speech (the text in italics) and then cut to Zinnemann referring to the accents, and then back to Mankiewicz talking about the booing. Stevens Jr. certainly had every right to use the anecdote, since a central participant, Mankiewicz, had confirmed that it occurred. It did, however, give the impression that Zinnemann was supporting the accents story. The documentary enjoyed a major launch in Hollywood, with celebrities such as Fred Astaire attending its premiere, and the accents anecdote entered Hollywood folklore.[15]

The simple truth is that the incident with the accents never took place, or at the very least, it went unrecorded in the transcript. Even Mankiewicz wrote on his own copy that it did not contain "DeMille reading some of the names such as V[]ilder, Tzinnemann, Vyler etc. in a clearly anti-Semitic accent." It may be an episode from another time or place or possibly uttered by another person, but it was not DeMille at the SDG meeting. Even if the stenographer had stopped recording at the precise moment that DeMille spoke with an accent, the anecdote is contradicted by other parts of the transcript. Later in the meeting, when DeMille was challenged about listing names he replied, "I mentioned no names." One of his opponents at the meeting, Vincent Sherman, supported him: "He didn't mention names." Sherman argued that DeMille implied that the twenty-five directors who supported Mankiewicz were subversive only by naming organizations of which one or more of them were members. The *Variety* journalist covering the meeting reported that DeMille did not name names, only that his associating people to subversive groups caused booing. Both Sherman and John Cromwell took offense at the insinuating tone with which DeMille spoke as well as at what he said; that may well be the origin of the anecdote. Further, DeMille always planned his speeches with extreme care. His copy of his speech, with his handwritten comments and marks showing where and when he intended to take his pauses and which words or phrases he would emphasize, shows no mention of any names of his opponents. The speech and the transcript vary little from each other. It is hard to come to any conclusion other than that, aside from some courteous references to Mankiewicz and a few others, DeMille mentioned no one by name.[16]

Possibly the basis for the accents story harked back to the House Un-American Activities Committee, or even before the Red Scare period, perhaps just before the United States entered the Second World War. HUAC representative John Rankin made similar attacks on Jewish film figures in Congressional speeches. Also on August 1, 1941, Dr. John H. Sherman, the president of Webber College, reported that Senator Gerald Nye spoke to the America First Committee and was "a disgrace to the Senate of the United States." Describing a Hitleresque attack on American Jews, Sherman noted that "deliberately, adroitly, with every trick of timing and inflection of voice, Nye accused the motion-picture industry of fostering pro-British sentiment, and then called a list of Jewish names associated with the motion-picture industry, drolly exaggerating their most Hebraic-sounding syllables." Nye reportedly paused to encourage the crowd to shout and hiss. Nye always vehemently denied the story, but the clear similarities between Wilder's account of DeMille at the SDG meeting in 1950—which Mankiewicz rolled into his own retelling—and the reports of this speech by Senator Nye at an isolationist rally in 1941 are too close to be a coincidence. Possibly tales about Nye and Rankin, which presumably had been doing the rounds in Hollywood for years, cross-pollinated with the retelling of the SDG meeting.[17]

Not a single confirmed participant at the SDG meeting supported the story. William Wyler, who spoke up at the meeting, pointedly omitted DeMille's supposed accents in his various reminiscences. If family accounts are correct, during the Second World War, Wyler—while in uniform—struck an officer for making an anti-Semitic remark. It is hard to imagine that a man of his character would make no statement of protest if DeMille had spoken in such an inflammatory manner. Wyler's lasting anger at DeMille was directed at his politics, not at his alleged use of accents. Robert Parrish, Eddie Salven, William Wyler, and Samuel Fuller did not mention the incident in their published accounts and interviews.[18]

Only the later interviews with Billy Wilder and the director Richard Fleischer—and a small mention by Vincent Sherman—backed Mankiewicz's claims about the accents. Neither Wilder nor Fleischer was recorded as speaking at the meeting, however, raising doubts they were even present. Wilder's other recollections are a little disjointed. Wilder could not even remember Mankiewicz being involved, and he also declared that John Huston had made a major speech that destroyed DeMille—when basically all Huston did was read out a newspaper article. Fleischer's version of events is no more reliable and does not even align with his autobiography, where he mentions the loyalty oath but does not discuss the SDG meeting or any role played by Cecil B. DeMille. Fleischer claimed to have voted against the loyalty oath and to have seen his name, along with the rest of the objectors, listed on the front page of the *Hollywood Reporter* as a result. If true, this claim means that DeMille and his group violated the confidentiality of the SDG voting process and released the names of political opponents to the media. Yet no edition of the *Hollywood Reporter* has been found to carry this list. Even the FBI files do not contain a list of names of those who voted against the loyalty oath. Sherman would make a reference to DeMille's "racism" in an interview with his son Eric in 2001, but surprisingly he never discussed his own prominent role.[19]

The accents anecdote was hard to kill. Mankiewicz told another newly embroidered version to Elia Kazan when the latter was writing his memoirs in 1984. Once again, he repeated his various claims about DeMille, and again he emphasized the McCarthyite investigations and anti-Semitic nature of his opponent. Mankiewicz added an anecdote about George Stevens telling DeMille, "By the way, C. B., when I was up to my ass in mud at Bastogne, how were the capital gains doing back home." Kazan accepted all of Mankiewicz's comments and printed the interview verbatim, aside from one short exchange where Mankiewicz said that DeMille called the twenty-five signatories "comrades." Kazan tried to confirm whether DeMille actually used the expression "comrades," and Mankiewicz admitted that he had not.[20]

The Directors Guild of America reinforced Mankiewicz's version when it released a documentary for the fiftieth anniversary of the Guild in 1987. The SDG meeting featured prominently as the Guild's direct response to the HUAC hearings. During his interview Mankiewicz retold his version of events and now added the line that DeMille referred to supporters of "Mankievicz." The narrator notes that Mankiewicz declared his strong opposition to the loyalty oath and that, in response, DeMille tried to have him "impeached," the use of the word providing another link back to the Watergate era. Former SDG president Robert Wise said the group wanted the anti-Communist oath halted. While it did not state so explicitly, the documentary gave the distinct impression that the loyalty oath had been stopped that night and it was a victory for the liberal forces of the Guild, with Mankiewicz the hero of the night. Now there were three documentaries covering the SDG meeting—the BBC's in 1981, George Stevens Jr.'s in 1984, and the DGA's in 1987. Each, along with the various interviews around that time, meant growing recognition for Mankiewicz. In addition, *Variety* published a major article in 1985 about the meeting, repeating much of Mankiewicz's version of events. Mankiewicz benefited in many ways, personally and publicly. After years of relative neglect, he began receiving a string of major awards, the DGA Lifetime Achievement Award in 1986 among them.[21]

The idea of a film about the meeting was floated by the director Richard Brooks, one of the signatories of the Mankiewicz petition, and the movie producer Catherine Wyler, the daughter of William Wyler, who began discussing the idea with David Puttnam, chairman of Columbia. However, it never got off the ground. In 1987 the DGA blocked access to its copy of the SDG meeting transcript. Explaining the action, the DGA said it was fearful of "embarrassing some living directors who attended the Oct 22, 1950 meeting." Even though this restriction was announced at the April 1987 Guild board meeting, Brooks was permitted to read the transcript, saying, "Some directors who were at the meeting are still alive, and some of them were on the wrong side." The obvious candidates were the DeMille supporters Clarence Brown, who was very ill and would die in August; Andrew Stone, who was in his late eighties; and Frank Capra, who was ninety at the time. The movie was never made. Brooks conceded that the subject may not have had strong commercial appeal and that, in addition, Puttnam had lost his executive position at Columbia.[22]

All the DGA accounts of the meeting are essentially reworkings of the Mankiewicz interviews. In 2006 the DGA journal published an article on the meeting, relying on the accounts from Parrish's book, Geist's biography, the DGA documentary, and Stevens Jr.'s documentary. For the DGA's seventy-fifth anniversary in 2011, this article was revised and the various documentaries reedited with a commentary by the director Clint Eastwood. The Mankiewicz interviews from 1967 through to 1987 had become the official version of events.[23]

Mankiewicz would play one last role in building the myth of the SDG meeting. Although the DGA has denied access to its archives, the Mankiewicz estate left all his documents to the Margaret Herrick Library in Los Angeles for scholarly study. All associated documents, such as the meeting transcript, newspaper articles, and letters, are now available for people interested in the field. Since he kept everything it seems that, at some level, Mankiewicz wanted the facts about the meeting told. He might have been the creator of the myth, but Mankiewicz may also be the person who leads to its dismantling.

6

Ford's Heroic Stand

John Ford emerged from the historical and critical debate about the October 22, 1950, Screen Directors Guild meeting as an American hero. He would be praised for his moral integrity, political courage, and common sense in defeating the dark forces of reaction in Hollywood. Ford's opening comment for his speech, the slight misquote "I make Westerns," would also come to define his approach to cinema. These ideas grew from the exultant way many books have depicted Ford's actions at the SDG meeting, based on the view that, at a critical stage of a vigorous debate, Ford intervened to defeat Cecil B. DeMille.[1]

Ford certainly opposed DeMille's actions. During the entire dispute Ford was a clear opponent of the blacklist. In key votes he stood with Joseph Mankiewicz against DeMille, arguing that the oath was unnecessary. In one sharp exchange Ford said he opposed "a police state" as much as Communism. At the same time, it is also perfectly clear that his politics were conservative and anti-Communist. His supporters at the SDG meeting, such as Douglas Sirk, noted that Ford was conservative, along with most of Hollywood, and Elia Kazan considered him to be reactionary.[2]

Writing in 1968, the film critic Andrew Sarris argued that Ford's reputation reached its pinnacle in the 1940s. British critics such as Lindsay Anderson, who was a film director in his own right, also championed his cause in the 1950s, seeing beyond what others considered to be "mundane Westerns." Even so, there was always some unease about his politics. Even his admirers were uncomfortable with his leading actor John Wayne's strong conservative stances. The future French new wave director and critic Jean-Luc Godard summed up the dilemma when he wrote in 1959 that he loved Ford's *The Searchers* (1956) but still found some difficulty with the film: "How can I hate John Wayne upholding Goldwater and yet love him tenderly when abruptly he takes Natalie Wood in his arms in the last reel of *The Searchers*."[3]

Building on French criticism of the 1950s, American writers began to revisit their nation's cinema to restore the reputation of their country's directors. Starting with his book simply called *John Ford* (1967), Peter Bogdanovich cemented himself as the director's champion. Andrew Sarris supported Bogdanovich with his book *American Cinema* (1968), which placed Ford in the pantheon of great directors. Sarris also warned that Ford would never be fashionable with left-wing ideological critics, a sentiment that Bogdanovich would later echo. In the 1970s some critics dismissed Ford's political positions, such as his support for the controversial Vietnam War. Russell Campbell wrote in a special edition of the *Velvet Light Trap* that Ford had worked on a propaganda film supporting U.S. policies in Vietnam but could not see that the harsh unfairness of the treatment of the Vietnamese was similar to that suffered by the Cheyenne, as depicted in his film *Cheyenne Autumn* (1964). In the same issue, the feminist critic Nancy Schwartz wrote that Ford presented women as inferior—possessions needing to be protected.[4]

Despite this type of criticism, Bogdanovich and Sarris would help reestablish Ford as one of the greatest directors of American cinema. Ford would be honored as an "American Poet" at the first American Film Institute Life Achievement Award in 1973. President Richard Nixon presented the award. Yet even while Ford was being feted by Nixon, thousands of demonstrators were outside the ceremony, led by the prominent actress and activist Jane Fonda, daughter of Henry Fonda, protesting against the Nixon administration. The resulting coverage of Ford mixing with President Nixon and John Wayne sent a message about his apparent conservative political values.[5]

Ford's role at the October 22, 1950, SDG meeting played little or no part in these critical debates of the 1970s. In 1978 Kenneth Geist argued that Ford performed "the role of conciliator." In 1979 Ford's grandson Dan, in his book *Pappy: The Life of John Ford*, provided another perspective on Ford's politics. Dan Ford believed his grandfather was not rigidly ideological but shifted his stance constantly. He depicted John Ford as being firmly on the left in the 1930s and being active in his support of Franklin D. Roosevelt in the presidential campaign of 1932. While he was an opponent of HUAC, Ford became more conservative as he grew older. Dan Ford did not mention the SDG meeting, but it would be present in almost every account from that point onward. The author Andrew Sinclair, who published his biography *John Ford* in 1979, reworked the Bogdanovich interview and the Robert Parrish account, arguing that the director was a peaceful man whose actions demonstrated his fundamental "authority and integrity." He did not involve himself in politics but would take a brave stand to support someone when required.[6]

Bogdanovich revisited Ford's role at the SDG meeting as part of a special series of biographies for *Esquire* magazine's golden anniversary in December 1983. The magazine featured fifty people chosen to represent the greatest figures in recent U.S. history. Bogdanovich noted that Ford came to be seen as highly conservative when he was directing films about military chivalry and honoring women in an intellectual climate that had shifted to an antimilitary and antifamily stance. His close relationship with the conservative John Wayne, with whom he made many films late in his career, caused his critical reception to decline with liberal film reviewers. Bogdanovich considered that it was a mistake to link Ford's politics with the views of his central actor, pointing out that it was equally incorrect to equate him to the liberal politics of the actor Henry Fonda, who also appeared in many of Ford's films. Ford was essentially apolitical. Nonetheless, Bogdanovich argued that the SDG meeting helped delineate his true outlook. He depicted the meeting as a bitter stalemate between Mankiewicz's supporters and DeMille's large group until the deadlock was broken by Ford. As an opponent of the oath, Mankiewicz was subjected to a smear campaign but was defended by Ford, who delivered him a vote of confidence.[7]

While Bogdanovich made a cautious connection between Ford's views and his actions at the SDG meeting, other critics would push the case far more strongly. In 1984 Lindsay Anderson, who had championed Ford for decades, used an extensive cut-and-paste of Parrish's long account of the meeting in his book on Ford, concluding that Ford was successful where liberals such as Stevens had failed. It was Ford who challenged DeMille and called on him to resign, wrote Anderson, winning because he dared to stand up to DeMille. According to Anderson, the liberals were led by Ford, but he did not share their politics. The image of Ford as the great political leader had thus begun to form.[8]

Two schools of thought had developed about the SDG meeting: the oral tradition promoted by Mankiewicz saw Ford as a heroic figure whose intervention caused DeMille to resign; Geist's 1978 interpretation of Ford as being more conciliatory was downplayed. The historian Ronald L. Davis even compared the meeting to a shoot-out at the O.K. Corral, with Ford entering the fight like a John Wayne figure. It is an odd comparison since it was Henry Fonda who had played Wyatt Earp in Ford's *My Darling Clementine* (1946). Ford's biographer Scott Eyman in 1999 quoted a little more of the transcript of Ford's speech, including "I admire C. B.'s guts and courage even if I don't agree with him. [And] if Mr. DeMille is recalled, your Guild is busted up." Then, in line with Mankiewicz's version of events, all of Ford's speeches were joined into one, giving the appearance that Ford attacked DeMille and then almost immediately afterward called for the board to resign. In accord with Lindsay Anderson, Eyman's belief was that Ford played a key role in DeMille's demise, being successful where the liberals had missed the mark.[9]

Other writers tried different ways to address some of the issues raised by the various writings about Ford. In 1997 the historian Garry Wills in his book *John Wayne's America* attempted to make sense of the inconsistency in Ford's membership in the Motion Picture Alliance for the Preservation of American Ideals and his opposing of DeMille at the SDG meeting. He concluded that Ford was a "Democratic cold warrior." Ford could oppose McCarthyism while also sanctioning the acts of President Harry S. Truman such as creating a list of subversive organizations. For Wills, Ford was a member of the "Cold War elite" who helped usher in these policies, particularly by his association with William "Wild Bill" Donovan, who helped set up America's intelligence services in the Second World War. An academic study of Ford's politics, by Brian Spittles in 2002, referred to the meeting briefly, saying that Ford actively opposed McCarthyism by defending the liberal Mankiewicz. However, Spittles disputed the claim that Ford was apolitical, arguing that he moved between conservatism and subversion—a position closer to the thinking of Dan Ford. He was "an inherently paradoxical character." One of Spittle's conclusions was that Ford's friendships with conservatives underlined how relaxed he was with their right-wing politics—although he did have a "genuine liberal streak."[10]

Joseph McBride gave the issue of Ford's political allegiance a far more comprehensive treatment in a major biography published in 2001. The work examined the various twists and turns of Ford's political allegiances, from the radicalism of the 1930s to the conservatism of the 1940s through to the 1970s. A commentary piece on the book described Ford's politics as "convoluted." McBride asked how a leader of a Hollywood labor organization in the 1930s could back conservatives such as Barry Goldwater and Richard Nixon as he grew older. Building on Wills's views of Ford being a "Democratic cold warrior," he looked at a much broader spectrum of Ford's political deeds. McBride noted Ford had joined the MPAPAI group's executive committee when John Wayne became president in March 1949, remained on it until 1955, and then stayed a member for five more years. He saw Ford as being quite conservative during this period. Regarding the SDG meeting, McBride saw Ford's opening statement about westerns as an important act of "self-definition" at a critical juncture of American history. McBride saw Ford as defending Mankiewicz against recall in the final part of his speech. McBride then wrestled with Ford's phone call and letter to DeMille after the meeting, arguing that he had backed away from the bold stand he had taken at the meeting.[11]

Other historians began to raise questions about Ford's supposed actions at the meeting. After McBride's biography was reviewed in the *London Review of Books,* another film historian and prominent writer on Ford, Edward Buscombe, commented that Ford did not launch a wholesale attack on DeMille and was certainly trying to stop a split in the Guild that could render it ineffective. In 2004 the film historian Robert Birchard in his book *Cecil B. DeMille's Hollywood* went further, noting that Ford actually saved DeMille from more humiliation.[12]

Despite the questioning, the heroic image of Ford remained widely entrenched. A PBS documentary on Ford and Wayne released in 2006, however, depicts the relationship between the two men in a different light. Here, the Cold War put them at different ends of the political debate. In the accompanying notes, the writer Ken Bowser says Ford's leading actors, John Wayne and Ward Bond, were members of the MPAPAI. Wayne is depicted as leading the anti-Communist forces, while Ford was attacking those powers in the form of DeMille.[13]

The SDG meeting is not the only example where historians and critics have suggested a different political orientation for Ford. During the preliminary HUAC hearings in March 1947, Eric Johnston, president of the Motion Picture Producers and Distributors of America, was quoted as saying that the industry would have no more *Grapes of Wrath* or *Tobacco Roads.* This comment implies that Ford was seen as a socially progressive filmmaker who was frowned upon in the conservative political environment created by HUAC. Johnston may well have said something along these lines, but in researching this book, it was not possible to access Johnston's testimony. A clue to the quote's actual origin, however, comes from Walt Horan, a Republican member of the House of Representatives at the House Appropriations Committee, who said, "We know there is quite a demand for 'Tobacco Road' and 'Grapes of Wrath,' on the part of the Russians, and so forth. Mr Eric Johnston, representing our responsible movie industry, has denied them those pictures and has said in effect, 'Here is a list of the pictures that you may have that are representative of the American people.'" More compellingly, the ambassador to the Soviet Union, Walter Bedell Smith, wrote to Johnston on August 7, 1947, approving of the measure to deny *The Grapes of Wrath* and *Tobacco Road* to the Russians unless "an equal number of films showing more favorable aspects of life in the United States were exported." The conclusion that Ford's liberal films were not being produced is highly questionable.[14]

Such is the power and attractiveness of the myth that historians have been unable to move far from it. To date, not one historian has used Ford's retort to DeMille's opponents that their accusations were "pretty un-American." Other aspects of Ford's role are simply not examined. Why, for example, didn't Ford sign the petition in support of Mankiewicz? If he was such a strong opponent of DeMille's, surely he would have been asked to sign. He had opposed DeMille at the board, but we have no record of whether he was asked to sign the petition or not, though it is unlikely that he would have signed it. Mankiewicz had initially followed Ford's advice not to call a general meeting, until DeMille forced his hand. Ford had secured Mankiewicz a vote of confidence on October 18, 1950. He did so to avoid public disunity. Most historians pin the voluntary oath on Mankiewicz, but Ford was appointed vice president after the SDG meeting, so he must have been involved in the subsequent discussions about introducing a voluntary oath. Since all Ford's actions throughout the affair were focused on resolving differences within the SDG, he may well have introduced the idea of a voluntary oath. The power of the John Ford mythology has not only led to a flawed history; it has closed off other lines of inquiry.

Regardless of the conflicting historical facts, John Ford came to be seen as a figure who stood up for American values when pressed at the SDG meeting. Despite being at odds with his actual behavior during the meeting, this image has become deeply rooted and has influenced critical responses. Writers such as Sam B. Girgus in *Hollywood Renaissance* (1998) would use this image to argue that Ford qualified as a liberal champion at the meeting while retaining his rugged argumentative individualism.

DeMille acted in concert with HUAC to purge the Guild of anyone with progressive political views, while Ford challenged the McCarthyite politics of the era and served in the navy during wartime. Girgus highlights Ford's role at the October 22, 1950, meeting to introduce his central argument that Ford was a key director and played a crucial role in creating a "cinema for democracy."[15]

A collection of essays titled *John Ford Made Westerns* (an obvious reference to Ford's famous opening line) also touches on the SDG meeting at a couple of points. The editors, Gaylyn Studlar and Matthew Bernstein, recount in their introduction that at the meeting DeMille accused Mankiewicz of "being a Communist"—something that never happened. They mention the statement "My name's John Ford. I make Westerns," claiming that Ford then called for a motion for DeMille and the board of directors to resign and asked that Mankiewicz be endorsed as president—so all the directors could "get some sleep." The statement reflected Ford's modesty as he had garnered many awards for his work. The editors conclude that his call was not politically motivated. Ford did not consider himself an artist or an ideologue. He was practical and needed his sleep to work the next day.[16]

The film scholar Jim Kitses saw Ford as the "Founding Father" of westerns, describing him as paving the way for the major directors Anthony Mann, Budd Boetticher, Sam Peckinpah, Sergio Leone, and Clint Eastwood. In his book *Horizons West* (2004), a chapter on John Ford discusses the loyalty oath debate and the blacklist era. He describes the statement "My name is John Ford. I am a maker of Westerns" as a possible tactic to deflate the self-important Cecil B. DeMille. Kitses downplays it as a simple statement of fact: Ford had made many westerns since the silent era. In contrast, John Marini, in an essay on Ford's epic westerns, thought that Ford's speech added to the recognition of westerns. Marini mentions that the manner in which Ford identified himself and his cinema was controversial among Hollywood directors. He refers to an interview from 1971 in which Douglas Sirk said there was a significant discussion among directors about Ford's statement. Sirk thought Ford was more famous for his nonwestern films such as *The Grapes of Wrath* (1940).[17]

It would be simplistic to argue that all critical or political discussion of Ford refers to the SDG meeting—a significant array does not. For example, most of the essays in the collection edited by Sidney A. Pearson Jr., *Print the Legend: Politics, Culture, and Civic Virtue in the Films of John Ford*

(2009), place no particular emphasis on the meeting. Even so, the SDG meeting remains the biographical incident that is referred to repeatedly in many critical articles on the director. It is used to support many differing critical judgments, mostly edging Ford toward the liberal or the apolitical camp. In contrast, other aspects of his film career that demonstrate his strong conservatism, such as his wartime documentaries *This Is Korea* (1951) and *Vietnam! Vietnam!* (1971), are rarely mentioned.

On one level Ford was being absolutely forthright with his statement about westerns, as at the time of the meeting he was making *Rio Grande* (1950), but it is important to note that it would be six years before Ford made another western, with *The Searchers* (1956). To argue that he was identifying himself and his art is to overanalyze what he was saying. Ford's statement was actually a little joke that caused some laughter in the room at a tense moment. It was also a gentle reminder to the people in the room that they were taking themselves a bit too seriously—perhaps he wanted to defuse the heated rhetoric.

While critics have used historical accounts to support their judgments, some historians have also used Ford's cinema to bolster their interpretations of his role at the SDG meeting. Ronald L. Davis's comparison of the SDG meeting to the shoot-out at the O.K. Corral creates an obvious mental link to Ford's film *My Darling Clementine,* while Andrew Sinclair saw an analogy with *Wagon Master* (1950). Ben Schwartz even drew a comparison between the meeting and *The Quiet Man* (1952). Yet the only Ford film that evokes the SDG meeting—and even then the reference is fleeting—is *Young Mr. Lincoln* (1939). Here, the young lawyer Abraham Lincoln stares down a mob out to lynch a murder suspect who is locked in a jail cell. By force of character, Lincoln calms down the group and breaks up the mob. In general terms, this is what Ford did at the SDG meeting. He waited until long into the evening when matters had spun out of control before returning what he considered to be common sense to the proceedings. Moreover, if there is one persistent theme that comes through in Ford's cinema, it is respect for ritual and for organizations. Ford aimed to preserve the SDG institution that existed to defend the working rights of directors. His real fear was that the Guild would crumble through internal dissension.[18]

Aside from political interpretations, to see the SDG general meeting on October 22, 1950, as Ford's triumph is also highly unfair to the group of twenty-five directors who supported Mankiewicz by signing the petition.

This was a brave political act in a dangerous environment. The twenty-five signatories threw down the gauntlet to DeMille, and Ford was not among them. This view of the meeting also ignores the many men who spoke with more vehemence against DeMille, such as William Wyler, John Huston, Don Hartman, and Rouben Mamoulian. A handful, including John Cromwell, Vincent Sherman, Michael Gordon, and Cy Endfield, would face the full brunt of a blacklist, and their brave stand did them no favors. Moreover, if anyone is to be singled out for having defeated DeMille at the SDG meeting, it should be George Stevens. Mankiewicz's recall had been defeated before the meeting was called to order, but Stevens's first speech, in which he resigned from the Guild, opened the door for Hartman to demand DeMille's own resignation. Ford resisted this move, but it was Stevens's second speech with its "little man" theme, arguing for a return to directors' business, that ended any hopes for DeMille's survival. It is not surprising that Stevens got into his car and drove deep into the night in triumph. In contrast, Ford wrote a letter of condolence to DeMille. It was Stevens who spent the week researching the background of the recall. It was Stevens, not Ford, who directly confronted DeMille and accused him of undemocratic maneuvers in back rooms. It was Stevens, not Ford, who tore DeMille apart at the SDG meeting.

Still, the myth cannot be entirely dismissed. Ford was a figure of integrity and unity, but not quite in the way he has been depicted. Ford had the integrity to stick with his friend DeMille when all others had abandoned him. Ford had not supported DeMille's policies, believing the Guild should focus on directors, not loyalty oaths. Ford watched his friend dig himself into a deeper and deeper hole during the recall of Mankiewicz. He used all his immense personal authority to stop DeMille from being dragged from office. When this course of action failed, he offered his own resignation—as part of the entire board—to ensure that the Guild would not break and to allow DeMille to go without losing face. The DeMille group had acted appallingly, but Ford neither sought revenge nor allowed Mankiewicz's supporters to act in a way that could potentially split the Guild by forcing a resignation. On the day after the meeting, Ford wrote to DeMille praising him for his stand, and he followed up with a phone call repeating his message of support. Ford stood by his friend and then worked as a conciliator to unify the Guild after the disruption. Like all myths, the Ford version has a kernel of truth.

7

DeMille as
Anti-Communist Ogre

Not only was Cecil B. DeMille disgraced at the October 22, 1950, Screen Directors Guild meeting for his efforts to remove Joseph Mankiewicz; in time he would be accused of every possible ultraconservative sin, including fascism and anti-Semitism. In the 1960s DeMille had a solid reputation as a filmmaker. In his book on American cinema published in 1968, Andrew Sarris placed DeMille in the second tier of directors, just below the venerated John Ford. Peter Bogdanovich's interview with Mankiewicz in 1967 extolling Ford's role had little immediate impact on DeMille's reputation. The Directors Guild of America journals of the period contain only a few polite mentions of DeMille, with no reference to the SDG meeting.[1]

Even so, his cinematic reputation was slipping, as his big-budget films were not in vogue and critical attention turned to smaller productions. Even DeMille's first major biographer, Charles Higham, favored his early silent films over what he considered to be the commercial crassness of his epics in the sound era. Higham did not even mention the SDG general meeting in his book *Cecil B. DeMille* (1973). Nonetheless, Higham's biography would strongly influence future coverage of the meeting. Higham believed that DeMille's foundation was focused on purging Communist elements, concluding that DeMille was leaning toward fascism by the 1950s. Writing to Robert Parrish two years after the release of Higham's biography, Mankiewicz built on these views and added that DeMille was supplying information to the Tenney Committee, Joseph McCarthy, and the House Un-American Activities Committee through his "Cecil B. DeMille Foundation for Americanism." When Parrish's own memoir was published, these claims became part of the historical record.[2]

Yet even a cursory investigation of the facts would have discovered that this precise foundation did not exist. The only possible organization Mankiewicz could have been referring to was the Cecil B. DeMille Foundation for Political Freedom, whose records show a clear and unrelenting focus on the "right to work" issue. While some of the foundation files are marked "Communists" and "Subversive Organizations," none contains any list of names as suggested by Higham. The relevant HUAC archive has one folder on DeMille with three items: two are newspaper clippings and a third is a letter about tax issues.[3]

DeMille certainly kept his distance from HUAC in the public arena. When committee member Karl Mundt invited senior figures in the film industry to comment on the scope of the committee's investigations in 1945, DeMille did not testify. He replied that HUAC should concentrate on stopping unions that imposed political assessments on its members—referring to the American Federation of Radio Artists' one-dollar fee, which DeMille bitterly opposed. When J. Parnell Thomas, the committee chair, asked DeMille to appear before HUAC on March 24, 1947, DeMille declined, citing work commitments, though he offered a statement that supported loyalty oaths along the lines of President Harry S. Truman's Executive Order. The directive made it compulsory for federal employees to sign a non-Communist loyalty oath. Even though DeMille's response said nothing of substance about the investigation, Thomas, who enjoyed the media spotlight, released the statement to the newspapers, which gave it scattered coverage in the media. When the HUAC public hearings were held in October 1947, other leading conservative Hollywood figures, such as Walt Disney and the actor Robert Taylor, testified. DeMille did not. DeMille kept only a minimal correspondence with HUAC over the remaining years.[4]

Concerning Senator Jack B. Tenney, DeMille donated $100 to the California legislator on two occasions. DeMille certainly cited the Tenney Reports when stating the political leanings of the petitioners for the SDG meeting on October 22, 1950. However, even with this behavior at the SDG meeting, nothing suggests any transfer of information by DeMille to Tenney about the personal details or political activities of other directors. DeMille's membership on the advisory committee of the Motion Picture Alliance for the Preservation of American Ideals and his support for Senator McCarthy would appear to back claims that he was a HUAC supporter. DeMille joined the right-wing group, but he had little involvement. Each invitation card sent to him over many months was returned, marked "regrets sent." He wrote to the committee when they wanted to renominate him that it was fine to do so, "if the alliance wants to put up for another year with a committeeman who is unable to attend meetings as often as he should." DeMille's name gave the MPAPAI some respectability, but he appeared to play no active role. It was a nominal membership indicating only a commitment to the organization's goals.[5]

DeMille was an active promoter of McCarthy. The senator had visited DeMille's film set and shared a lunch with the director at least once. Henry Wilcoxon, DeMille's one-time actor and associate producer, recalled being asked at this lunch to spy for HUAC at Guild and social functions—an offer he declined. (Wilcoxon's memory is probably faulty as McCarthy had little to do with HUAC, but he may well have been asked to provide information to the FBI.) Wilcoxon then turned down DeMille's request to have McCarthy for dinner, as his wife, Joan, refused to even consider having "that man in my home." When he was attacked by people for issuing public statements of support for McCarthy, DeMille responded, "Honest and loyal Americans differ in their opinions of Senator McCarthy. I think he is a brave man, fighting for America and against Communism. You do not like him. The voters of Wisconsin have decided between your opinion and mine." Again, there is no documented evidence of DeMille providing McCarthy with information. The DeMille family steadfastly insists that DeMille did not like McCarthyism. They may have confused HUAC with McCarthy, which was a common error. It is also possible that DeMille, like many other Republicans, abandoned McCarthy in later years. Yet he was certainly a supporter of the man and his policies at least until 1952.[6]

Mankiewicz's charge that DeMille's foundation was involved with Tenney, McCarthy, and HUAC appears to be unfounded. Yet DeMille was indirectly involved with HUAC through his close association with the FBI. In his memoir, DeMille's publicity assistant Phil Koury recalled frequent conferences with FBI agents, with staff then sent on mysterious missions. Released under the Freedom of Information Act, the Cecil B. DeMille FBI files show a role that went far beyond tacit support. After the bombing of Pearl Harbor in December 1941, DeMille first approached the FBI, offering to set up an information-gathering unit in the film industry and promising to "organize, direct, and finance" it. Hoover was depicted in the FBI's official history as having "staunchly resisted super patriotic attempts to recreate the vigilante system of World War I." The formal response said that Hoover deeply appreciated the "very generous and patriotic offer made by DeMille but at the present time it does not seem necessary."[7]

The bureau declined DeMille's initial offer on December 13, 1941. However, on December 22 Special Agent in Charge Richard B. Hood and Inspector W. E. Gurnea visited DeMille to inform him they would be grateful for any information from his network in the film industry. DeMille would set up a series of contacts throughout Paramount, but no official connection existed with the FBI. The bureau's director, J. Edgar Hoover, wrote to Hood to "emphatically point out that this is a most important contact," and he instructed his staff to make every endeavor "to seek out as many subjects and situations as possible, which can be properly and adequately handled by Mr DeMille and his associates." In January 1942 DeMille turned over a list of names, which formed the base of "a system of confidential informants within . . . [Paramount] studio." DeMille was designated "special service contact" and over the following months organized dozens of business figures, journalists, socialites, and merchants into working as confidential FBI informants.[8]

The information provided to the FBI by DeMille and his network would have long-term consequences. As early as August 31, 1942, for example, DeMille provided intelligence on his fellow director Herbert Biberman and the writer John Howard Lawson. In 1945 he would report on the writers Dalton Trumbo and Alvah Bessie. These four would be among the Hollywood Ten in the 1947 HUAC investigations. Without this type of behind-the-scenes Hollywood informing, the HUAC investigation would have failed or indeed might never have happened. The SDG general meeting on October 22, 1950, slowed down DeMille's contribution, but that contribution never stopped. By 1951 DeMille was providing information on people served with subpoenas to appear before the committee. The FBI noted: "Through his contact with industry organizations and national political personalities, this source has been in a position to make available considerable confidential information of value concerning the action to be undertaken by the industry and government agencies with regard to the ferreting out of Communist and subversive elements." DeMille kept the FBI informed of internal Guild affairs for many years. Even when deposed, DeMille regularly furnished "information concerning the activities of Guild members whom he believes may be Communist Party members or Communist Party sympathizers."[9]

Yet when HUAC came to Hollywood in March 1947, DeMille refused to testify. The film historian Robert Birchard suggests that DeMille might not have wanted to attract scrutiny of his own film career. DeMille had made one film about the Russian Revolution, *The Volga Boatman* (1926), and had toured the USSR after making *The Godless Girl* in 1929. At one point, reportedly, he considered making a version of *War and Peace* for the Soviet government. Even DeMille hinted in his autobiography that he was politically naive. The reality was that DeMille was a key FBI source who was a friend of Hoover's, and their correspondence contained a regular exchange of polite letters celebrating wedding anniversaries, birthdays, and awards. His FBI file states, "No derogatory information concerning this individual appears in the files of this office." His FBI handlers observed, "Mr DeMille has been exceedingly cooperative with this office and through his business and financial connections can furnish valuable assistance to this office." Because of his relationship with Hoover, DeMille was effectively exempt from any form of FBI inquiry and therefore also any HUAC investigation. DeMille certainly did not shy away from testifying to Congress on right-to-work legislation in 1948.[10]

Higham's and Mankiewicz's allegations that DeMille's foundation hunted down liberals are unfounded but not unjustified. Probably based on the sketchiest of rumors, these claims certainly contain an element of truth. DeMille limited the role of the foundation to right-to-work issues. His own personal role in delivering information to the FBI was a different matter. He left only the slimmest evidence in his own files, and he did not even mention it in his autobiography. It was a duty done without recompense or recognition of any sort. No film historian noted DeMille's role as an FBI informant until his biographer Scott Eyman did so in 2010. This is odd, as the FBI files, which document his role in some detail, have been accessible since the late 1970s, and it was mentioned by historians of the FBI in the 1980s.[11]

In spite of his role as an FBI informant, DeMille's other actions during the Red Scare years cut across the claim that he was a supporter of HUAC and the blacklist. The actor Edward G. Robinson was cleared by HUAC on January 10, 1951, but he found enormous difficulty in gaining work in the film industry—he was on the graylist. Robinson was a progressive Hollywood liberal, but not a Communist. His being denied work sent a powerful message to others in the film industry about the dangers of political action. DeMille employed Robinson and the graylisted composer Elmer Bernstein on his film *The Ten Commandments* (1956). The work revived both men's careers when the blacklist and graylist were in full force. When Robinson told DeMille of his graylisting, Robinson said, DeMille analyzed the issue in dispassionate terms and then offered him the role—a move that restored Robinson's self-respect. DeMille took the same approach with Bernstein. Yet even this notable hiring of graylisted people is undermined by Henry Wilcoxon's belief that DeMille refused to employ the actor Burt Lancaster, who had been falsely accused of Communism. The DeMille family, however, argue that DeMille later seriously considered Lancaster for the role of Moses in *The Ten Commandments,* seeing him as a great actor.[12]

In 1947 DeMille had committed himself to a loyalty oath and ensured SDG officeholders took it. A year later, in a speech to the Economic Club of Detroit, he stated: "Some may think the Taft–Hartley Act takes care of Communists in certain unions. The Taft–Hartley Act had gone a long way in showing up the known Communists in certain unions. But the hidden Communists can perjure themselves without blinking an eye. And the fellow travelers who can take the Taft–Hartley oath without perjury are often more dangerous than the card holders in the Communist Party itself."[13] Yet in 1950 he expected the entire SDG membership to adopt a similar oath to ensure that the organization was free of Communists. At the SDG DeMille was prepared to create a blacklist for screen directors while denying it was even happening. In his speech at the October 22 meeting, DeMille named some organizations but not specific people, even though he had that information with him in the files he had carried there. He knew that linking people to Communist fronts in that political environment was the same as calling people Communists. Yet something kept him from taking the more drastic step. At some level these actions suggest he disapproved of HUAC. DeMille was often an intemperate man given to wild outbursts or managerial tantrums, but people also speak of his kindness and generosity. His actions in employing graylisted people underline his sense of personal loyalty.

DeMille's actions and beliefs do not paint a clear picture. He joined the MPAPAI, which aided HUAC, but he did not participate to any great extent. He refused to testify to HUAC but provided information through the FBI. He released a marginally supportive statement to J. Parnell Thomas in March 1947, which, on closer reading, really only supported Hoover in his quest for loyalty oaths, and he attacked HUAC in November. He then reversed his position and defended HUAC with vigor at a producers' meeting a few days later. His campaign against the American Federation of Radio Artists was similar in many ways to Mankiewicz's alleged protest against the SDG board introducing loyalty oaths for individual members. In one case he argued that a union could not force actions on an individual member, while at the SDG, he aimed to defeat Mankiewicz for expressing a dissenting view.

It would seem that his rigid conservative ideology drove him in one direction, while his personal affiliations tugged him the other way. The tension between the two forces caused him a great deal of distress. At one point at the SDG meeting, he cried out in exasperation and bewilderment, "I would like to say that there were good friends of mine on that committee [that signed the petition]."[14] He said this having just attacked the same people for their left-leaning politics. His defeat at the meeting disconcerted DeMille, and his reports to the FBI became less frequent. However, he never entirely stopped. It may be that his work with the major films *The Greatest Show on Earth* (1952) and *The Ten Commandments* now consumed his time, but it is equally possible that he lost heart after his public chastisement at the SDG meeting, or simply regretted it. His actions and statements show how conflicted he was between personal relationships and his political views throughout the Red Scare period.

In the 1980s another set of vicious accusations would amplify the chorus of disapproval for DeMille and his role at the SDG meeting: he was accused of anti-Semitism. Even though these claims were patently false, they would cause even greater damage to DeMille's reputation than his reported relationship with HUAC. The story was repeated by many historians and remained unchallenged until Robert Birchard took issue with it in his book *Cecil B. DeMille's Hollywood,* published in 2004, arguing that such a speech was out of character and unlikely, particularly given DeMille's working relationship with Wilder and his own Jewish heritage. Birchard was interviewed in 2004 by the film historians Kevin Brownlow and Patrick Stanbury for a two-hour documentary about DeMille called *American Epic.* For their treatment of the SDG meeting, the filmmakers presented a section of Mankiewicz from the 1987 DGA documentary, counterbalanced with DeMille's granddaughter Cecilia deMille Presley querying the claims about DeMille's rudeness.[15]

After the documentary was released, Brownlow gained access to the meeting transcript in 2008. What he read prompted him to consider changing his 2004 documentary about DeMille. He told an interviewer,

Christine Leteux, that "everybody" had confirmed that DeMille had picked up the list of the twenty-five petitioners and said: "How interesting some of these names such as Zinnemann, Wilder, Wyler." Brownlow said it had become "one of the standard Hollywood stories when the Directors' Guild of America made a film about themselves." He further stated, "Rouben Mamoulian stands up and says: 'For the first time, I am ashamed of my accent. I always thought I was an American but now I realise.' . . . And these men, after all, were story tellers and they did exactly what DeMille did in his history films. They bend history a little bit to make it work as showmanship. So to make the story work, they've taken that accent thing from Mamoulian and put it on to DeMille. As a result, we are going to have to change the sequence in the documentary."[16]

The anti-Semitism claim would be dismissed altogether when Scott Eyman reconsidered the accents anecdote in his biography of DeMille in 2010. Eyman argued that there were three possibilities for the rumor and dealt with each in turn. The first possibility, the idea of a flawed transcript, he rejected. He then suggested that DeMille had possibly engaged in the activity beforehand at a separate meeting, but he did not provide any evidence that this occurred, implicitly dismissing the idea. The third possibility, which Eyman believed to be more likely, was that flawed memories of Mamoulian's apology about his accent were subsequently transmuted into a dubious anecdote that suggested anti-Semitism. His analysis signaled that the accents story was finally to be discarded.[17]

Film historians may have shifted in their coverage, but charges of fascism linked to anti-Semitism would begin to taint DeMille's critical reputation. When *The Ten Commandments* came out at the time of the Suez crisis, many Jewish people saw it as a vindication of Israel. DeMille actually saw Moses as a figure unifying the adherents of three monotheistic religions of Judaism, Christianity, and Islam against the real threat of Communism. Writing before Mankiewicz made his anti-Semitic accusations public, Patricia Erens argued that DeMille's biblical epics such as *The Ten Commandments* commented on the anguish of the Jewish people and their optimism for a future in the state of Israel. After Mankiewicz's claims began to circulate, the critical climate shifted and some scholars attacked even the biblical epics as anti-Semitic. In his extended discussion about *The Ten Commandments*, Alan Nadel in his book *Containment Culture* (1995) linked the film both to DeMille's ambivalence about his Jewish ancestry and to an account of the SDG meeting. Nadel repeated the false claims about the Cecil B. DeMille Foundation delivering names to HUAC. He accused DeMille of being a producer of "falsity," then associated the meeting with other flaws. He noted Robinson was the only Jewish actor to play a major character in the film: Charlton Heston and John Derek were American heroes, while Robinson plays the Jew who worships the golden calf and must be purged. Nadel did not even acknowledge any pro-Zionist message in the film. He argued that in the film, the reclaimed Israel was not a Jewish homeland but only a projection of American power, aimed at securing oil.[18]

In terms of politics, DeMille was seen in more and more extreme terms. The film historian Andrew Bergman in his book *We're in the Money: Depression America and Its Films* (1971) raised some ideological concerns about DeMille and his film *This Day and Age* (1933). Bergman focused on the uncomfortable scene of a group of students lowering a gangster into a pit full of rats with their student leader proclaiming, "We haven't got time for any rules of evidence." He argued that the rhetoric of the publicity material indicated a mob mentality, then quoted a review that linked it to a Nuremberg rally. While Bergman did not consider DeMille to be a Nazi, for him the film could be read as containing fascist sentiments. In their study *The Hollywood Social Problem Film* (1981), published in a darker critical climate, Peter Roffman and Jim Purdy presented a far more sinister case about *This Day and Age*. Roffman and Purdy compared DeMille's depiction of students with the Hitler Youth, linking it to *Triumph of the Will* (1934), Leni Riefenstahl's fascist documentary of the Nuremberg rally with its marchers and patriotic song. The authors argue DeMille only stops short of actually demanding "a police state."[19]

The impact of this type of negative critical comment was to place DeMille's reputation on the lowest rung throughout the 1980s and 1990s. There were no sharp rebukes or scathing reviews. Sumiko Higashi's book *Cecil B. DeMille: A Guide to References and Resources* (1985) lists three references to his cinema in 1981, four in 1982, four in 1983, three in 1984, and one in 1985. Considering two are newspaper articles and two are unpublished works, this borders on neglect. When he was mentioned, DeMille was simply dismissed. For example, Sam B. Girgus in *Hollywood Renaissance* (1998) condemned DeMille's role at the SDG meeting and was contemptuous of his cinema, describing his westerns with Gary Cooper as foolish, racist, and presenting a closed ideological system at odds with the democratic values of Ford and other directors. In the main, DeMille was just ignored.[20]

During this period of neglect, Al Rogell, DeMille's political ally at the SDG meeting, attempted to rewrite the history of the SDG meeting. He told interviewers that DeMille had been informed by a highly placed but unidentified source that McCarthy was about to investigate Hollywood; the oath was an attempt to forestall that investigation. This explanation appears to be unlikely as the overriding reason for DeMille's commitment to the loyalty oath at the SDG was his desire for a strong industry statement against Communism. Newspaper statements by Rogell at the time show this clearly; he told journalists that the SDG was a leader and he hoped other guilds would follow its example. The available SDG board minutes contain no discussion of any planned investigation by McCarthy or HUAC, and neither DeMille's nor Rogell's statements at the meeting mention it. If Rogell's claim that HUAC or McCarthy was planning to investigate was true, why wasn't the board informed of the possible investigation? Rogell's version of events means that he and DeMille lied to the media, the board, and the membership at every stage of the dispute. It is possible that DeMille was concerned about the chance of another HUAC investigation of the SDG and that he used the oath to clean its house in order to forestall this. He might have mentioned this to Rogell, but it is not documented in any known source.[21]

Despite their inaccuracy, vivid reports of DeMille's anti-Semitism and his links to HUAC and McCarthy have meant that historical accounts of the SDG meeting have been particularly severe over time to DeMille. The director's large body of work became swamped by coverage of the meeting, and since he was already falling out of favor, this would feed into a wholesale dismissal of his work. His reported actions at the meeting would eventually define him as the unacceptable face of American conservatism, and this image would help undermine his cinematic reputation.

DeMille's relatives and supporters rallied to challenge these negative images, and they are now conducting a different campaign based on the image of a Hollywood pioneer. In 1985 the rediscovery of the set of the 1923 version of *The Ten Commandments* buried under desert sands certainly provided a catalyst for his reputational recovery.[22] The filmmaker Peter Brosnan and the archaeologist John Parker found the set, and their discovery was an enormous news event, helping revive interest in the original version of *The Ten Commandments* as most people were only aware of the remake in 1956. The impact on DeMille's reputation was profound, coinciding as it did with the arrival of a new generation of directors, such as Steven Spielberg, attracted to epic films. Interest in DeMille has grown since that point, particularly examining his long career dating back to 1914. A more nuanced view is developing, but the SDG meeting still darkens his reputation.

The coverage of DeMille's actions shows how an image can develop its own momentum. Sociologists such as Gary Fine in his work on reputations have shown how communities create the reputations of villains. Once stigmatized as a villain, all aspects of a person's career are depicted as evil.[23] DeMille was a Cold War conservative, but he was neither a fascist nor an anti-Semite. Yet once Higham had depicted him as leaning toward fascism in the early 1970s and Mankiewicz had distorted his role at the SDG meeting, his image became akin to that of the despised Joseph McCarthy—with an anti-Semitic edge. The slur opened the door for a dismissal of his entire cinematic output.

While he has not deserved so much vitriol, some of the strong criticism of DeMille's role at the SDG meeting remains justified. With his black-and-white view of the world, DeMille could not see that the proposed loyalty oath would have led to a Guild-sanctioned blacklist. He did not understand that his opponents might have a valid point about the effect of the loyalty oath, brushing aside Mankiewicz's plea for a meeting to explain the policy to its members. Similarly, he acted with indecent haste and with disregard for any sense of fairness in his attempt to discard Mankiewicz when he suspected his opponent of talking to the media. Even after discovering his error, when his own supporters conceded they were wrong, DeMille found it impossible to make a minor compromise or to apologize. At the SDG meeting, his inability to see the alternative perspective led him to link his opponents to suspected subversive organizations, which helped seal his fate. DeMille's greatest opponent at the SDG meeting was not John Ford, George Stevens, or Joseph Mankiewicz. DeMille was the architect of his own downfall.

Conclusion

Hollywood's blacklist is one of the ugliest chapters in cinematic history. Talented people in the American film industry had their careers destroyed, and lives were ruined. It is a painful part of the history of the United States, and it is difficult to comprehend the combined impact of the House Un-American Activities Committee, the blacklist, and the loyalty oaths. The film industry is still struggling with it. On October 27, 1997, to commemorate fifty years since the HUAC investigations, the American Federation of Radio and Television Artists, the Directors Guild of America, the Screen Actors Guild, and the Screen Writers Guild presented a program called *Hollywood Remembers the Blacklist*. In that program, the Directors Guild of America president, Jack Shea, officially restored the membership of Herbert Biberman, one of the Hollywood Ten. Biberman had been expelled from the Screen Directors Guild after he finished serving a five-month prison sentence for contempt of Congress. He applied to return to the Guild in 1952, but the board of directors refused, arguing that it contravened Guild by-laws about Communist Party membership. The restoration of his membership was a brave step by the Guild, which had honestly reflected on its history and attempted to redress a past wrong. Even after fifty years, it was a divisive event. One of the few living members of the Hollywood Ten, director Edward Dmytryk, who eventually testified to HUAC, refused to attend, calling an apology to Communists "silly."[1]

Many historians and film critics would do well to take similar steps. The SDG general meeting on October 22, 1950, has become something of an oft-told tale. By elevating the story of the meeting to that of an epic clash of political wills between industry titans, historians have transformed it into a political pantomime. They have created a version of events where participants are either heroes or villains, reducing them to cardboard cut-outs. The reality was far less clear-cut.

The myth of the SDG meeting did not arise from an overarching conspiracy. The historian Edward Steers warned in *Blood on the Moon* (2005), his revisionist account of the Lincoln assassination, that the story of the killing was often told and "replowed" along the same paths.[2] Early historians make an error that is integrated into later works. The stories are repeated so many times that they take on the cover of historical truth, which leads to further misconceptions. The SDG meeting was a members' backlash against the leadership style of DeMille prompted by the high-handed methods used to attempt a recall of Mankiewicz. The historical replowing, however, has created a series of interrelated myths. Ford actually failed in his initial attempt to keep DeMille on the board, and he was genuinely supportive of DeMille at the meeting and in other circumstances. No documented evidence exists that DeMille's foundation had any direct involvement with the Tenney Committee, Senator Joseph McCarthy, or HUAC, or that it handed over political dossiers to them. DeMille certainly never spoke at the meeting in an offensive or mocking Jewish accent. Besides a few angry outbursts at meetings, Mankiewicz did not lead any effective opposition to the loyalty oath, although he probably did not support it. Along with Ford, he did, however, oppose a version of the blacklist, at some professional risk.

Those myths have constructed images of the key players. When viewing the films of Ford, do we envision him rising in righteous American anger to castigate the McCarthyite DeMille? Are we tempted to see him as an aging right-wing figure, or as the liberal Democrat who produced *The Grapes of Wrath*? When we consider Mankiewicz's cinema, do we see a talented writer-director who set Hollywood ablaze with his wit and genius in the 1950s, or the director whose reputation was savaged by *Cleopatra,* who was stricken with writer's block and at odds with the film industry in his twilight years? When we look at DeMille's cinema, do we think of him as an anti-Semitic McCarthyite or as a Hollywood pioneer whose energy and drive helped forge the greatness of Paramount Studios and who entertained millions with his films for more than forty years? Quite often writers have chosen the most attractive image of their favored director and have concentrated on that image to the exclusion of others, while downplaying any evidence to suggest their interpretation might be wrong or at least questionable.

Drawing on dubious accounts of the SDG meeting and other incidents, Ford's biographers and critics have helped fashion the image of an admirable cultural icon. An overwhelmingly positive view of his role in the meeting has been extended to all his politics and cinema. This image downplays concerns about his conservatism, including his support for the Vietnam War, Barry Goldwater, and the Nixon presidency. Likewise, the Mankiewicz version of events at the SDG meeting helped to reduce a highly complex individual with a difficult political and personal history to a symbol. Ford's image has given critics permission to embrace him, even though the politics of the man and his cinema were well out of step with a more liberal film establishment.

A far different critical and biographical picture has emerged for DeMille, whose reputation was savaged by the handling of the SDG meeting. The depiction of DeMille as someone leaning toward fascism had wide-ranging implications for his critical standing. DeMille was transformed in the public eye from a director of enjoyable and popular large-scale epics into a loathsome ultraconservative bully. It is not enough that DeMille was humiliated and compelled to resign at the meeting; his entire cinematic output has been condemned as well. DeMille is attacked as a politically and artistically backward director who made poor films.

Mankiewicz finds his legacy stuck between his two fellow directors. His actions throughout the SDG meeting can at least be defended as being intended for the greater good of the organization. When the conflict came to a head, DeMille wielded every advantage, but Mankiewicz trumped him at every turn. The language of Mankiewicz's speech to the SDG meeting was a model of logic combined with tact and diplomacy, a point acknowledged by DeMille. Mankiewicz demonstrated tremendous personal courage, poise, determination, and integrity throughout the SDG debate over the loyalty oath issue. It is quite possible that his actions stopped a Guild-sanctioned blacklist. It was a chapter of his life of which he could be justly proud. He stood against a powerful industry figure in DeMille, who had abused his position, and scored a clear victory.

Yet at some point in the mid-1970s Mankiewicz felt that the story was boring people. The narrative needed embellishing; like a dull script, it needed a rewrite. He misremembered a whole series of anecdotes to increase the impact of his tale. Mankiewicz was an intelligent man and a fine writer, and he used his ability to create a fresher and more exciting chain of events. Mankiewicz had reshaped the story to suit a conventional Hollywood narrative. He offered a simple story with the surprise at the end: John Ford declaring his support. The dull and messy reality of a meeting where the bad guy is finished before he even walks into the room is not much of a story. There is no suspense in it. Mankiewicz fashioned a conventional story out of the available material, and his version was adopted despite all of the facts.[3]

So why didn't anyone refute Mankiewicz's narrative? Surely there was more than one director alive who knew his embellishments were unfounded. In some cases, doubts were certainly raised. When the researcher Susan Winslow discussed Ford's intervention with John Huston in 1983, she got a sharply contrasting view to Mankiewicz's version of events. She asked him whether strong words were spoken by Ford to DeMille. Huston replied, "No, no, no. Jack [John Ford] didn't say anything like that. . . . He went on to express shock, as though DeMille hadn't really understood what he was doing, you know, he was amazed and he'd been a friend of DeMille's and he was in a way trying to say, 'Oh, DeMille, jeez you're on the wrong track.'"[4]

The main reason it was not refuted was that no one could accurately remember what really happened. Memory loss begins within hours of an event occurring, and it accelerates as people grow older, particularly when they reach their sixties and seventies. The major interviews recollecting the SDG meeting took place almost thirty years after the event, with interviewees in these age brackets. Fred Zinnemann realized this was a problem and apologized to George Stevens Jr. in 1982: "I wish I could remember some anecdotes but even that is difficult, you know it's so long ago." He added, "I heard Ford got up and said, 'I'm a director. I direct horses,'" a misquote of Ford's famous self-introduction.[5]

These oral accounts are valuable, even though they are inherently unreliable and disjointed. They convey the emotion, particularly the anger, toward DeMille over his actions. There is no uncertainty about Mankiewicz's and Zinnemann's attitude to DeMille—they despised him. The emotional power of George Stevens's second speech, with its reference to looking out for the little man, was also clearly remembered—even if the context is lost. Samuel Fuller in an autobiography published in 2002 recalled the meeting as an election and described why he voted for Mankiewicz. Given it was written more than fifty years later and is wildly inaccurate, it also shows an astonishing recall of Mamoulian's gripping speech about his new life in America, which Fuller paraphrases with some accuracy. That emotional memory may also underpin the sheer ferocity of the stories.[6]

Conclusion

Historians have warned about the "contamination" of oral history, and the historian Anthony Beevor has recommended using only contemporary sources to overcome the problem of misremembering.[7] However, there are times when oral accounts are all that exist and historians have no choice but to use them. This being the case, biographers and chroniclers would do well to be wary when consulting oral recollections and to use them with circumspection, keeping in focus the motives of the speaker. Historians must be skeptical of all sources if they are to provide accounts that are as balanced and accurate as possible. The way the SDG meeting has been depicted is seriously flawed because of its reliance on oral recollections.

In response to the blacklist, Hollywood became fearful and divided. The way the SDG meeting of October 22, 1950, was remembered by its participants became almost therapeutic, providing a comfortable and reassuring vision of an industry and individuals who fought effectively against McCarthyism—at least in one instance. In times of fear, people and institutions do and say things that they later regret. They put up all sorts of elaborate mental defenses for these same acts and create all sorts of justifications. This has proved the basis for a deeply flawed history, which has influenced perceptions of Ford, DeMille, and Mankiewicz, along with many other important directors in American cinema. If we are to come to terms with the blacklist, it is time to put aside the heroic interpretation of the Screen Directors Guild meeting of October 22, 1950, and start to reconsider a more complex and nuanced version of events.

Acknowledgments

I would like to acknowledge the support of the Australian Academy of the Humanities for their award under the 2016 Publication Subsidy Scheme. Such schemes help writers establish their careers, and it is a great initiative.

I would also like to acknowledge the efforts of Geoff Mayer and Hester Joyce at La Trobe University in helping me develop the origins of this book from a very sketchy idea. I greatly appreciate their support over a long period.

Emeritus Professor John Salmond read and commented on an early draft. It is sad that Professor Salmond died before the book was published, as his approach to history underpins it. In a much earlier period, Professor Rhys Isaac provided many ideas about the hysteria of the McCarthyite period and the way people reflected back on it. I thank both of these excellent historians for their enthusiasm in encouraging me in my work. They are both missed, but their influence continues.

Rick Thompson, with his massive knowledge of John Ford, also assisted greatly in the initial stages of the book.

An early version was read by Brian Neve at the University of Bath, Professor Steven J. Ross at the University of Southern California, and Professor Richard Maltby at the University of Flinders. Their comments and criticisms were greatly valued.

I would particularly like to thank James V. D'Arc, curator at the Arts and Communications Archive, Harold B. Lee Library, Brigham Young University, and Barbara Hall at the Margaret Herrick Library in Beverly Hills for their help while I was studying at their archives in the United States.

Thank you to all my diligent proofreaders: my colleague Karen Morath; my mother, Tricia Hannigan; and Vicki Pyle, who all proofread a previous draft to within an inch of its life. Mark Bennett completed the French translations. Alison Strumberger, Michelle Manly, and Lisa Cropman provided their valuable copyediting and proofing skills at differing stages. Liz Smith provided an additional special polish. Any remaining errors are all mine.

Anne Dean Dotson, Patrick O'Dowd, and Bailey Johnson from the University Press of Kentucky were highly supportive to a first-time writer. Patrick McGilligan provided tremendous editorial guidance.

My partner, Patricia Matthews, read all the drafts at every stage, and her support and encouragement were invaluable. My daughter, Emily, may now understand what I was doing on the computer all that time.

Notes

Introduction

1. Thomas F. Brady, "Hollywood Divided by Loyalty Pledge Issue," *New York Times*, October 22, 1950.

2. The formal title of the Screen Directors Guild is the Screen Directors' Guild, but it is almost never used. The House Un-American Activities Committee, or HUAC, is a common abbreviated form for the Committee on Un-American Activities, House of Representatives. Reisch quote from Kenneth L. Geist, *Pictures Will Talk: The Life and Films of Joseph Mankiewicz* (New York: Scribner, 1978), 190–91. See also Neil Sinyard, "Red Menace: Reflections on the Hollywood Blacklist during the era of HUAC and McCarthy," Keswick Film Festival, February 13–15, 2004. Ford's quote was more likely to be "My name is John Ford. I am a director of westerns." It is often paraphrased as "I make westerns."

3. Robert Sherwood, "Hollywood Zeus," *New Yorker*, November 28, 1925.

4. The American Federation of Radio Artists became the American Federation of Television and Radio Artists in 1952. The federation issue is discussed in Robert S. Birchard, *Cecil B. DeMille's Hollywood* (Lexington: University Press of Kentucky, 2004), 329–30.

5. Ford quote from Robert Vaughn, *Only Victims: A Study of Show Business Blacklisting* (New York: G. P. Putnam, 1972), 65; Dan Ford, *Pappy: The Life of John Ford* (Englewood Cliffs, NJ: Prentice Hall, 1979), 74; "COMPIC and Correlation Summary Report," February 18, 1943, John Ford file, January 4, 1955, FBI; Dorothy M. Brown, *Mabel Walker Willebrandt: A Study of Power, Loyalty, and Law* (Knoxville: University of Tennessee Press, 1984), 233; Frank Capra, *The Name above the Title: An Autobiography* (New York: Vintage Books, 1985), 266–67.

6. Robert Coughlan, "15 Authors in Search of a Character Named Joseph L. Mankiewicz," *Life*, March 12, 1951, 158–73; reprinted in Brian Dauth, ed., *Joseph L. Mankiewicz: Interviews* (Jackson: University Press of Mississippi, 2008), 3–19 (quote on p. 11).

7. Nancy Lynn Schwartz and Sheila Schwartz, *The Hollywood Writers' Wars* (New York: Knopf, 1982), 36, 264.

1. The House Un-American Activities Committee Arrives in Hollywood

1. Michael Sragow, *Victor Fleming: An American Movie Master* (New York: Pantheon Books, 2008), 61; William C. de Mille, *Hollywood Saga* (New York: E. P. Dutton, 1939), 194–97. Leslie Midkiff DeBauche argued that while the American Protective League was meant to be focused on pro-German elements, it monitored unions. Leslie Midkiff DeBauche, *Reel Patriotism: The Movies and World War I* (Madison: University of Wisconsin Press, 1997), 31. See also Joan M. Jensen, *The Price of Vigilance* (Chicago: Rand McNally, 1969); Steven J. Ross, *Hollywood Left and Right: How Movie Stars Shaped American Politics* (New York: Oxford University Press, 2011), 3.

2. *Hollywood Reporter,* April 15, 1943; "Report to Director on Communist Infiltration in Motion Picture Industry," September 6, 1942, Communist Infiltration—Motion Picture Industry (COMPIC), file no. 100-138754, FBI (hereafter COMPIC); J. Edgar Hoover to SAC [Special Agent in Charge] Los Angeles, April 29, 1944, COMPIC.

3. February 18, 1943 (sympathetic quote), July 10, 1943 (Michael Curtiz material), February 18, 1943, and January 4, 1955 (John Ford and Fritz Lang material), COMPIC; John Huston file, June 9, 1949, FBI; February 5, 1943 (FBI belief that the majority were not Communists), COMPIC.

4. Joint Fact Finding Committee on Un-American Activities to the Fifty-Fifth Legislature, 1941, 78–79, quoted in Hedda Hopper file, FBI; Neil Gabler, *An Empire of Their Own: How the Jews Invented Hollywood* (New York: Anchor, 1989), 380; article quoted in Landon G. Rockwell, "Book Reviews," *American Political Science Review* 47, no. 1 (1953): 211.

5. MPAPAI declaration, *Hollywood Reporter,* February 7, 1944; *Daily Variety,* February 7, 1941; Schwartz and Schwartz, *The Hollywood Writers' Wars,* 206.

6. Athan G. Theoharis, *The FBI and American Democracy: A Brief Critical History* (Lawrence: University Press of Kansas, 2004), 89; Kenneth O'Reilly, *Hoover and the Un-Americans: The FBI, HUAC, and the Red Menace* (Philadelphia: Temple University Press, 1983), 89–92; Testimony of J. Edgar Hoover before HUAC, March 26, 1947, Digital History, http://www.digitalhistory.uh.edu/disp_textbook.cfm?smtID=3&psid=3632 (accessed April 20, 2016).

7. Testimony of Sam Wood, October 20, 1947, *Hearings Regarding the Communist Infiltration of the Motion Picture Industry. Hearings before the Committee on Un-American Activities, House of Representatives, Eightieth Congress,* October 20–30 (Washington, DC: U.S. Government Printing Office, 1947), https://archive.org/stream/hearingsregardin1947aunit/hearingsregardin1947aunit_djvu.txt (accessed November 22, 2014) (hereafter *Hearings*); *New York Times,* October 21, 1947; Lar-

ry Ceplair and Steven Englund, *The Inquisition in Hollywood: Politics in the Film Community, 1930–60* (Champaign: University of Illinois Press, 2003), 209–10.

8. George Stevens, John Ford, Merian C. Cooper, John Huston, George Sidney, and William Wyler to the Chairman of the Investigating Committee of Congress, October 20, 1947, John Huston papers, Margaret Herrick Library, Academy of Motion Picture Arts and Sciences, Beverly Hills, California (hereafter MHL); Joseph McBride, *Searching for John Ford: A Life* (New York: St. Martin's, 2001), 465; SDG board meeting minutes, October 21, 1947, quoted in Scott Eyman, *Print the Legend: The Life and Times of John Ford* (New York: Simon and Schuster, 1999), 375–77; McBride, *Searching for John Ford,* 466–67.

9. Testimony of John Howard Lawson, October 27, 1947, *Hearings.* Footage of the testimony is available on YouTube: Authentic History Center, "Howard Lawson HUAC Testimony Excerpt, 1947," uploaded November 22, 2010, https://www .youtube.com/watch?v=F7W3XbDZqO4 (accessed April 30, 2016).

10. Testimony of Herbert Biberman, October 27, 1947, *Hearings.*

11. Testimony of Edward Dmytryk, October 27, 1947, *Hearings*; Alan Casty, *Robert Rossen: The Films and the Politics of a Blacklisted Idealist* (Jefferson, NC: McFarland, 2013). A list of people named by Rossen is included in Vaughn, *Only Victims,* 288.

12. Testimony of Louis J. Russell, October 27, 1947, *Hearings.*

13. Frank Tuttle HUAC testimony, 1951, quoted in McBride, *Searching for John Ford,* 463. Compare Testimony of Edward Dmytryk, April 25, 1951, to the Committee on Un-American Activities, in Eric Bentley, *Thirty Years of Treason: Excerpts from Hearings before the House Committee on Un-American Activities, 1938–1968* (New York: Thunder's Mouth/Nation Books, 2002), 382.

14. *Washington Post,* October 23, 1947; *New York Daily Mirror,* October 23, 1947; *Washington Post,* October 31, 1947, all featured in collected media coverage in COMPIC; Memo to Clyde Tolson, October 29, 1947, COMPIC; Guy Hottel, SAC Washington, to J. Edgar Hoover, October 30, 1947, COMPIC; Thomas quoted in Gordon Kahn, *Hollywood on Trial: The Story of the Ten Who Were Indicted* (New York: Boni and Gaer, 1948), 132. Kent's comment featured in his syndicated column, "The Great Game of Politics," in many newspapers across the United States, such as the *Louisville-Kentucky Courier Journal,* November 1, 1947.

15. FBI report, November 8, 1947, COMPIC; John Huston, *An Open Book* (New York: Knopf, 1980), 133; Humphrey Bogart, "I'm No Communist," *Photoplay,* May 1948, 53–54.

16. John Cogley, *Report on Blacklisting,* vol. 1, *Movies* (New York: Fund for the Republic, 1956), 3; Cecil B. DeMille, "The Motion Pictures and International Relations," speech to the Commonwealth Club, San Francisco, November 7, 1947, The Commonwealth Club, https://www.commonwealthclub.org/taxonomy/term/469/ all?page=1 (accessed April 26, 2016); *San Francisco News,* November 7, 1947,

DeMille Scrapbooks, The Cecil B. DeMille Archives; Film/Music Archives; L. Tom Perry Special Collections, Harold B. Lee Library, Brigham Young University, Provo, Utah (hereafter CBDM); DeMille discussion in FBI report on Producers Meeting, December 5, 1947, COMPIC.

17. Marilyn Ann Moss, *Giant: George Stevens, a Life on Film* (Madison: University of Wisconsin Press, 2004).

18. FBI report, June 9, 1949, John Huston file, FBI. See also Mark Harris, *Five Came Back: A Story of Hollywood and the Second World War* (New York: Penguin, 2014), 279–83.

19. Harris, *Five Came Back,* 363.

20. Wilder was also widely quoted to have said of the Hollywood Ten: "Of the ten, two had talent, and the rest were just unfriendly." I have not been able to find a source for this quote, but it is certainly the type of humor employed by Wilder.

21. *The Grapes of Wrath* had already been singled out as subversive by conservative magazines such as *Time*: "Cinema: The New Pictures," February 12, 1940. FBI report quoting Sergei Eisenstein, "The Purveyors of Spiritual Poison: About the Contemporary American Cinema," *Culture and Life,* July 31, 1947, COMPIC; "Spotlight on Hollywood," October 9, 1947, Box 212, Folder 1, CBDM; Testimony of Sam Wood, October 20, 1947, *Hearings,* 60.

22. FBI report, December 19, 1947, COMPIC.

23. FBI report, December 19, 1947, COMPIC. DeMille's name is partially redacted in the FBI reports, but given several accounts of his actions at the meeting from participants such as Dmytryk and Huston, it is reasonably certain that it is him. Edward Dmytryk, *Odd Man Out: A Memoir of the Hollywood Ten* (Carbondale: Southern Illinois University Press, 1996), 95; Huston, *An Open Book,* 135.

24. Some confusion exists about dates, with FBI sources saying December 5, while newspapers place the meeting on December 3. Birchard, *Cecil B. DeMille's Hollywood,* 343; *Hollywood Reporter,* December 2, 1947, quoted in Ceplair and Englund, *The Inquisition in Hollywood,* 339; FBI report, January 15, 1948, COMPIC.

25. FBI report, January 15, 1948, COMPIC; "Anti-Reds Sweep 20 of 21 Offices in SWG Election," *Hollywood Reporter,* November 21, 1947, quoted in Donald T. Critchlow, *When Hollywood Was Right: How Movie Stars, Studio Moguls, and Big Business Remade American Politics* (New York: Cambridge University Press, 2013), 101; Ceplair and Englund, *The Inquisition in Hollywood,* 339.

26. For a discussion of the dynamics of Hoover's appointment, see Curt Gentry, *J. Edgar Hoover: The Man and the Secrets* (New York: Norton, 1991), 125. Willebrandt was featured in *Time,* August 26, 1929. "Biographical data for Mrs Mabel Walker," April 21, 1955, Mabel Willebrandt file, FBI.

27. FBI report, July 19, 1948, COMPIC; Cecil B. DeMille, "While Rome Burns," address to the Economic Club of Detroit, Michigan, April 19, 1948, Cecil B. DeMille file, FBI.

28. *New York Times,* February 1, 1949; Election ticket, Box 1210, Folder 11, CBDM.

29. Lawson v. United States, Trumbo v. United States, argued February 24, 1949, decided June 13, 1949, Nos. 9872, 9873, United States Court of Appeals District of Columbia Circuit (176 F2d 49). See, for example, Ceplair and Englund, *Inquisition in Hollywood,* 297–98.

2. The Origins of the Screen Directors Guild Meeting

1. Joseph McCarthy, "Speech at Wheeling, West Virginia," February 9, 1950, http://www.advances.umd.edu/LincolnBirthday/mccarthy1950.xml (accessed January 14, 2016).

2. *Los Angeles Evening Herald & Express,* May 15, 1950, and *Hollywood Citizen-News,* May 15, 1950, in Randy Roberts and James S. Olson, *John Wayne: American* (Lincoln: University of Nebraska Press, 1995), 339–40; American Business Consultants, *Red Channels: The Report of Communist Influence in Radio and Television* (New York: Counterattack, 1950), 9.

3. Cecil B. DeMille to J. Parnell Thomas, March 24, 1947, Box 1154, Folder 10, CBDM.

4. "Meeting of the Senior Directors of the Screen Directors Guild," October 22, 1950, Beverly Hills Hotel, Beverly Hills, California, Joseph L. Mankiewicz papers, MHL (hereafter SDG Minutes, October 22, 1950), 41.

5. Joseph McBride, *Frank Capra: The Catastrophe of Success* (New York: Simon and Schuster, 1992), 570, 604.

6. McBride, *Frank Capra,* 563; FBI report, August 13, 1950, COMPIC; Affidavit of Mabel Walker Willebrandt in support of Motion to dismiss the intervention of Radio and Television Directors Guild, September 19, 1950, National Labor Relations Board Case No. 21-RC-1377, File 100-340922, FBI; Mabel Walker Willebrandt to J. Edgar Hoover, September 21, 1950, File 100-340922, FBI.

7. SDG Minutes, October 22, 1950, 11–12; Statement of Board of Directors of Screen Directors Guild of America, August 24, 1950, Box 1210, Folder 10, CBDM.

8. FBI report, August 13, 1950, COMPIC; Fred Zinnemann to SDG, undated letter, Fred Zinnemann papers, MHL.

9. SDG Minutes, October 22, 1950, 8–10.

10. SDG Minutes, October 22, 1950, 11–16; *New York Times,* September 24, 1950.

11. Kenneth L. Geist, *Pictures Will Talk: The Life and Films of Joseph L. Mankiewicz* (New York: Scribner, 1978), 180. Other parts of the speech are quoted in *Variety,* September 15 and 20, 1950, in Cheryl Bray Lower and R. Barton Palmer, *Joseph L. Mankiewicz: Critical Essays with an Annotated Bibliography and a Filmography* (Jefferson, NC: McFarland, 2001), 192–93. Cecil B. DeMille, "Crusade for Freedom," speech to workers at Paramount Studios, September 27, 1950, Box 212, Folder 1, CBDM.

12. SDG Minutes, October 22, 1950, 18–19. Ford would make a similar statement at the SDG meeting on October 22, 1950. In the transcripts of the SDG Minutes, October 22, 1950, Mankiewicz made a point of not naming people who talked at the board meetings. It was a protocol followed by DeMille, who did not mention any individual by name. Parts of the minutes of the original board meetings, which do mention names at some points, are available from the DeMille and Mankiewicz archives, so it is possible to determine who said what, but in some cases it is still an educated guess.

13. SDG Minutes, October 22, 1950, 19–20.

14. Mankiewicz and Ford quotes from October 18 SDG board meeting in D. Hayne to Cecil B. DeMille, October 21, 1950, Minutes of SDG Board, Box 1210, Folder 10, CBDM. Mankiewicz never disputed the quote in subsequent debates. Cooper is not named directly in the SDG Minutes, October 22, 1950, 21, but after interviewing Mankiewicz, Kenneth L. Geist, in *Pictures Will Talk,* 182, argues that he is the person concerned.

15. SDG Minutes, October 22, 1950, 23–24.

16. SDG Minutes, October 22, 1950, 23–26. Ford is not named directly in the minutes, but it is difficult to see who else it may have been. Mankiewicz said it was a director he greatly revered. It is unlikely that it was anyone from the DeMille camp, which really only leaves Ford or Stevens. Working quietly behind the scenes to settle things down was more Ford's way of operating. Capra also certainly believed it was Ford who dissuaded Mankiewicz. Frank Capra to the SDG board members, November 1, 1950, Box 1210, Folder 10, CBDM.

17. Frank Capra to the SDG board members, November 1, 1950, Box 1210, Folder 10, CBDM.

18. "SDG Schism on Blacklist," *Daily Variety,* October 11, 1950. The message "Mankiewicz will not sign oath" is a subhead. Stevens telegram mentioned in Geist, *Pictures Will Talk,* 183.

19. SDG Minutes, October 22, 1950, 155–56; John Huston interview for the documentary *George Stevens: A Filmmaker's Journey* (1984), George Stevens: A Filmmaker's Journey Special Collection, MHL. The list of fifty-five erased names has never been established, but in 1947 the FBI was also supplied with a list of DeMille's opponents, "who may not be communist" but appeared to vote in block to defeat the "American" supporters of DeMille. This group of about forty people included Curtis Bernhardt, John Berry, Herbert Biberman, Phil Carson, Jules Dassin, Edward Dmytryk, Peter Godfrey, Henry Hathaway, Alfred Hitchcock, Elia Kazan, Herbert Kline, Zoltan Korda, Anatole Litvak, Lewis Milestone, Jack Moss, Irving Reis, Jean Renoir, Robert Rossen, Victor Saville, Vince Sherman, Orson Welles, Billy Wilder, and William Wyler. FBI report, December 19, 1947, COMPIC.

20. Frank Capra to the SDG board members, November 1, 1950, Box 1210, Folder 10, CBDM.

21. Night letter to all Screen Directors Guild members, October 13, 1950, Box 1210, Folder 10, CBDM; Geist, *Pictures Will Talk,* 187.

22. Hartman's role is referenced in Schwartz and Schwartz, *The Hollywood Writers' Wars,* 261, and Stephen Vaughn, *Ronald Reagan in Hollywood: Movies and Politics* (Cambridge: Cambridge University Press, 1994), 125, 130. SDG Minutes, October 22, 1950, 52–55. A copy of the petition is reprinted in Robert Parrish, *Growing Up in Hollywood* (London: Bodley Head, 1976), 202. Stevens and Kazan are mentioned in "25 Directors in Support of Joseph Mankiewicz who signed petition calling for General Membership Meeting," Box 1210, Folder 10, CBDM, which has information based on an article in *Variety,* October 16, 1950.

23. Parrish, *Growing Up in Hollywood,* 206–7; Michael Cieply, "The Night They Dumped DeMille," *Los Angeles Times,* June 4, 1987.

24. SDG Minutes, October 22, 1950, 105–7; Thomas F. Brady, "Hollywood Divided by Loyalty Pledge Issue," *New York Times,* October 22, 1950.

25. Thomas F. Brady, "Hollywood Divided by Loyalty Pledge Issue," *New York Times,* October 22, 1950; SDG Minutes, October 22, 1950, 32, 91.

26. Joseph Mankiewicz interview with Susan Winslow, August 14, 1981, for *George Stevens: A Filmmaker's Journey,* George Stevens: A Filmmaker's Journey Special Collection, MHL; Frank Capra to the SDG board members, November 1, 1950, Box 1210, Folder 10, CBDM; "Joint statement of Recall Committee and Mr. Mankiewicz," Box 1210, Folder 10, CBDM.

27. SDG Minutes, October 22, 1950, 49; Frank Capra to the SDG board members, November 1, 1950, Box 1210, Folder 10, CBDM; *Los Angeles Times,* October 16, 1950.

28. Donald Hayne to DeMille, October 21, 1950, Box 1210, Folder 10, CBDM.

29. Thomas F. Brady, "Hollywood Divided by Loyalty Pledge Issue," *New York Times,* October 22, 1950.

30. Speech of Cecil B. DeMille to Screen Directors Guild, Box 1210, Folder 10, CBDM; Geist, *Pictures Will Talk,* 190. Martin Gang's law firm would later be labeled "pinko" by Willebrandt. Mabel Walker Willebrandt to Grace Kessler, March 16, 1979, quoted in Brown, *Mabel Walker Willebrandt,* 235.

3. The Screen Directors Guild Meeting

1. SDG Minutes, October 22, 1950, 1–4.

2. SDG Minutes, October 22, 1950, 3–4, 12.

3. It is possible that the eight-hour time difference between California and France also played a part. Mankiewicz may have left early on August 17 in France before the meeting was called in California on the evening of August 16. Al Rogell to Joe Mankiewicz, August 16, 1950, quoted in SDG Minutes, October 22, 1950, 7, 9–10.

4. SDG Minutes, October 22, 1950, 12–13.

5. SDG Minutes, October 22, 1950, 18–23, 26–29.

6. SDG Minutes, October 22, 1950, 34.

7. SDG Minutes, October 22, 1950, 39. The text of his original speech in the Cecil B. DeMille Archives has the correct form, "neither to praise Caesar nor to bury him." Speech of Cecil B. DeMille to Screen Directors Guild, Box 1210, Folder 10, CBDM.

8. SDG Minutes, October 22, 1950, 39–40. See also Speech of Cecil B. DeMille to Screen Directors Guild, Box 1210, Folder 10, CBDM.

9. SDG Minutes, October 22, 1950, 41–44. The minutes actually say "graven collars," which is an unlikely expression from DeMille. The original speech from the Cecil B. DeMille Archives says "craven cowardice." Speech of Cecil B. DeMille to Screen Directors Guild, Box 1210, Folder 10, CBDM. The stenographer is recording at speed, and there are a few phonetic spellings in the text. Mankiewicz corrected the words on his copy of the minutes, and his changes reflect what DeMille is likely to have said.

10. SDG Minutes, October 22, 1950, 44–45. The speech says "men who join this Guild." Speech of Cecil B. DeMille to Screen Directors Guild, Box 1210, Folder 10, CBDM.

11. SDG Minutes, October 22, 1950, 45–46.

12. SDG Minutes, October 22, 1950, 46–47. Frank Capra, another member of the recall committee, would later state emphatically that the media reports drove the recall. Frank Capra to members of the SDG Board of Directors, November 1, 1950, Box 1210, Folder 10, CBDM.

13. SDG Minutes, October 22, 1950, 47; Speech of Cecil B. DeMille to Screen Directors Guild, Box 1210, Folder 10, CBDM. The text of DeMille's speech says "Troubled waters attract strange fishermen," but the transcript says "strange specimens," which is a clear transcription error.

14. Eddie Salven's account in Henry Wilcoxon and Katherine Orrison, *Lionheart in Hollywood: The Autobiography of Henry Wilcoxon* (Metuchen, NJ: Scarecrow, 1991), 201–2; SDG Minutes, October 22, 1950, 47–48. The transcript text says "and injure." Mankiewicz amended it to "from injury," but DeMille's speech notes have "an injured." William Wyler's comment in Axel Madsen, *William Wyler: The Authorized Biography* (New York: Crowell, 1973), 304. Sherman and Cromwell in SDG Minutes, October 22, 1950, 112–14, 119.

15. SDG Minutes, October 22, 1950, 48–49, 92. Later in the meeting DeMille would also second the motion to empower the board to destroy the ballots.

16. SDG Minutes, October 22, 1950, 51–52; Reynold Humphries, *Hollywood's Blacklists: A Political and Cultural History* (Edinburgh: Edinburgh University Press, 2010), 72, 82; Jack Warner to John Cromwell, October 15, 1945, Box 6, Folder 10, Jack Warner Collection, quoted in Gerald Horne, *Class Struggle in Hollywood, 1930–1950: Moguls, Mobsters, Stars, Reds, and Trade Unionists* (Austin: University of Texas Press, 2001), 165, 292n63.

17. Schwartz and Schwartz, *The Hollywood Writers' Wars,* 261; Vaughn, *Ronald Reagan in Hollywood,* 125, 130; SDG Minutes, October 22, 1950, 52–55.

18. Schwartz and Schwartz, *The Hollywood Writers' Wars,* 248, 265; SDG Minutes, October 22, 1950, 55–58.

19. SDG Minutes, October 22, 1950, 58–61.

20. SDG Minutes, October 22, 1950, 61; "List of Political Affiliations of 25 directors in support of Mankiewicz," Box 1210, Folder 10, CBDM.

21. SDG Minutes, October 22, 1950, 61–65. See also notes for SDG meeting, John Huston papers, MHL.

22. SDG Minutes, October 22, 1950, 65–67.

23. SDG Minutes, October 22, 1950, 68–69.

24. SDG Minutes, October 22, 1950, 70–71.

25. SDG Minutes, October 22, 1950, 71–72.

26. SDG Minutes, October 22, 1950, 72–73.

27. SDG Minutes, October 22, 1950, 73–81.

28. SDG Minutes, October 22, 1950, 83–84; Parrish, *Growing Up in Hollywood,* 209.

29. SDG Minutes, October 22, 1950, 83–84, 92–98; Testimony of Leo McCarey, October 22, 1947, *Hearings*; "Draft of final speech of My Son John," Box 439, Folder 10, CBDM.

30. SDG Minutes, October 22, 1950, 99–103.

31. SDG Minutes, October 22, 1950, 103–11.

32. The transcript records the name of Ballbusch. None of the signatories' names are remotely similar to Ballbusch, with the possible exception of Robert Parrish, who spoke later. Peter Ballbusch directed montage sequences for many films, so he could have been an SDG member, but it is unlikely. He could have exaggerated his role, or the name could have been incorrectly transcribed.

33. SDG Minutes, October 22, 1950, 111–12.

34. SDG Minutes, October 22, 1950, 112–14.

35. SDG Minutes, October 22, 1950, 114–16; FBI report, July 15, 1949, COMPIC.

36. SDG Minutes, October 22, 1950, 117–19. The transcript spells the name Seider, but there appears to be no director of that name. The Internet Movie Database (http://www.imdb.com/name/nm0147749/) has a Ralph Ceder who was a director from the 1920s onward, and this appears to be the person referred to in the transcript.

37. SDG Minutes, October 22, 1950, 119–20; Vincent Sherman, *Studio Affairs: My Life as a Film Director* (Lexington: University Press of Kentucky, 1996), 244–46.

38. SDG Minutes, October 22, 1950, 121.

39. SDG Minutes, October 22, 1950, 121–24; Brian Neve, *The Many Lives of Cy*

Endfield: Film Noir, the Blacklist, and Zulu (Madison: University of Wisconsin Press, 2015). Brian Neve, personal communication to author, April 27, 2016.

40. SDG Minutes, October 22, 1950, 124–26.

41. SDG Minutes, October 22, 1950, 128.

42. Wilcoxon and Orrison, *Lionheart in Hollywood,* 201–2. He is often slightly misquoted as saying, "My name's John Ford. I make westerns." The misquote came from Mankiewicz in an interview with Peter Bogdanovich for his book on Ford, *John Ford* (London: Studio Vista, 1969), 19. The actual comment—"My name is John Ford"—is not recorded in the transcript, but George Seaton is recorded as introducing himself in this way. All speakers had to give their name, and few are recorded doing so. Ford was also recorded as saying he was "against an invitation of a blacklist," a clear transcription error that Mankiewicz corrected with "initiation."

43. SDG Minutes, October 22, 1950, 129–31.

44. SDG Minutes, October 22, 1950, 131.

45. SDG Minutes, October 22, 1950, 131–33.

46. SDG Minutes, October 22, 1950, 136–37.

47. SDG Minutes, October 22, 1950, 148–50.

48. SDG Minutes, October 22, 1950, 154–55.

49. SDG Minutes, October 22, 1950, 159, 161.

50. SDG Minutes, October 22, 1950, 162.

51. SDG Minutes, October 22, 1950, 171. Parrish recollection in Barry Norman, *The Film Greats* (Oxford: ISIS, 1985), 206–7; Robert Wise quoted in *50 Years of Action* (dir. Douglass Stewart), documentary for DGA Golden Jubilee, 1987; George Stevens quoted in *George Stevens: A Filmmaker's Journey* (dir. George Stevens Jr., 1984).

4. The Aftermath

1. Mabel Willebrandt to Cecil B. DeMille, October 24, 1950, Folder 1210, Box 10, CBDM; McBride, *Frank Capra,* 579; SDG Minutes, October 22, 1950, 171; *Hollywood Reporter,* April 9, 1999; James Ulmer, "A Guild Divided," *DGA Quarterly,* Spring 2011, http://www.dga.org/Craft/DGAQ/All-Articles/1101-Spring-2011/Feature-Loyalty-Oath.aspx (accessed February 6, 2014).

2. SDG Minutes, October 22, 1950, 26, 96–97; *Variety,* October 26, 1950, quoted in Geist, *Pictures Will Talk,* 205.

3. Frank Capra to the SDG board members, November 1, 1950, Folder 1210, Box 10, CBDM; Joseph C. Youngerman, *My Seventy Years at Paramount Studios and the Directors Guild of America,* based on interviews by Ira Skutch and David Shepard (Los Angeles: Directors Guild of America, 1995), 84.

4. D. Hayne to Cecil B. DeMille, October 28, 1950, Folder 1210, Box 10, CBDM; Douglass K. Daniel, *Tough as Nails: The Life and Films of Richard Brooks*

(Madison: University of Wisconsin Press, 2011), 62; Parrish, *Growing Up in Holly-wood*, 201–2; Victor S. Navasky, *Naming Names* (London: Penguin, 1991), 181.

5. Joseph Mankiewicz to Nicholas Schenck, May 8, 1952, Joseph Mankiewicz file, FBI. Schenck passed the letter on to the FBI. SDG Minutes, October 22, 1950, 96. The oath is mentioned in, for example, Navasky, *Naming Names*, 181; Alan Casty, *Communism in Hollywood: The Moral Paradoxes of Testimony, Silence, and Betrayal* (Lanham, MD: Scarecrow, 2009), 175; McBride, *Searching for John Ford*, 484; Scott Allen Nollen, *Three Bad Men: John Ford, John Wayne, Ward Bond* (London: McFarland, 2013), 218; Critchlow, *When Hollywood Was Right*, 103; Harris, *Five Came Back*, 441.

6. SDG Minutes, October 22, 1950, 114; Dmytryk, *Odd Man Out*, 95.

7. Dmytryk, *Odd Man Out*, 149; Enclosure to letter from John Huston to un-named person, January 29, 1953, John Huston file, FBI.

8. Geist, *Pictures Will Talk*, 206. At least until 1953, Willebrandt was a regular correspondent with J. Edgar Hoover, naming the twenty-five who supported Mankie-wicz and singling out H. C. Potter, Fred Zinnemann, George Seaton, and Mark Rob-son to the FBI director. Mabel Walker Willebrandt to J. Edgar Hoover, May 11, 1953, FBI file 123-11385, Serial 21; *Variety*, March 21, 1951, quoted in Larry Ceplair and Steven Englund, *The Inquisition in Hollywood: Politics in the Film Community, 1930–60* (Champaign: University of Illinois Press, 2003), 370; "An Interview with Black-listed Director Vincent Sherman!," posted by Troma, December 11, 2011, YouTube, https://www.youtube.com/watch?v=eV99RJ9B9Gs (accessed July 15, 2015).

9. John Rich, *Warm Up the Snake: A Hollywood Memoir* (Ann Arbor: Univer-sity of Michigan Press, 2006), 87–89; *New York Times*, October 19, 1965; Younger-man, *My Seventy Years*.

10. Wilcoxon and Orrison, *Lionheart in Hollywood*, 201; Phil Koury, *Yes, Mr. DeMille: A Humorous and Candid Appraisal of an Extraordinary Showman* (New York: Putnam, 1959), 303; Cecil B. DeMille to Clarence Brown, October 23, 1950, Box 1210, Folder 1, CBDM.

11. FBI report, November 14, 1950, COMPIC. It is not possible to determine the identities of T-14, T-22, and T-23 as the names are erased. Richard Hood to J. Edgar Hoover, November 25, 1950, Cecil B. DeMille file, FBI. DeMille also gave details of the Motion Picture Industry Council's efforts to establish an industry-wide loyalty oath. Joseph Mankiewicz file, FBI; Richard Hood to J. Edgar Hoover, December 16, 1954, Cecil B. DeMille file, FBI.

12. John Ford to Cecil B. DeMille, October 23, 1950, and transcript of phone conversation between John Ford and Cecil B. DeMille, October 24, 1950, Box 1210, Folder 10, CBDM.

13. Dick L'Estrange to Cecil B. DeMille, October 23, 1950; Mabel Willebrandt to Cecil B. DeMille, October 24, 1950; Cecil B. DeMille to Dick L'Estrange, October 23, 1950; Cecil B. DeMille to John Ford, October 23, 1950, Box 1210, Folder 10,

CBDM. DeMille was also nominated for the Academy Award for best director in 1952 for *The Greatest Show on Earth.*

14. DGA Awards for 1953, IMDb, http://www.imdb.com/event/ev0000212/ 1953?pf_rd_m=A2FGELUUNOQJNL&pf_rd_p=2275328022&pf_rd_ r=08T67J22A5D5HKD350G5&pf_rd_s=right-1&pf_rd_t=15091&pf_rd_ i=directors-guild&ref_=ac_ac_ac_dga_eh_lk63 (accessed April 25, 2016); Cecil B. DeMille and Donald Hayne, *The Autobiography of Cecil B. DeMille* (London: W. H. Allen, 1960), 113; Youngerman, *My Seventy Years,* 91; Rich, *Warm Up the Snake,* 87–88; SDG Board Meeting minutes, June 13, 1950, Box 1210, Folder 11, CBDM; McBride, *Searching for John Ford,* 428. DeMille also openly enjoyed receiving awards, and Ford would have been aware of DeMille's unease over never winning the New York Critics Award, which Ford had won, as well as his long neglect in terms of Academy Awards, of which Ford would win six. DeMille had broadcast far and wide his disquiet at the lack of recognition.

15. *Los Angeles Times,* January 30, 1953, quoted in Jeremy Byman, *Showdown at High Noon* (Lanham, MD: Scarecrow, 2004), 23. Depending on the calculation used, *The Ten Commandments* is either first or third. It grossed $43 million, and its nearest rival was *Ben-Hur* (1959) with $36 million, according to figures based on U.S. rentals—but not box office grosses. "All Time Film Rental Champs," *Variety,* January 14, 1981. Based on box office grosses, *The Ten Commandments* took in $80 million, gaining third rank, and *The Greatest Show on Earth* was ranked seventh with $36 million.

16. *New York Times,* December 6, 1966.

17. Leo Hurwitz, Lee R. Bobker, Robert Braverman, Gene Searchinger, Darrell Random, and Hilary T. Harris, on their own Behalf and on Behalf of all others similarly situated as members of the Screen Directors International Guild, Appellants, v. Directors Guild of America, Incorporated, Appellee, argued April 12, 1966, decided July 14, 1966, No. 329, Docket 30215, United States Court of Appeals Second Circuit.

18. Geist, *Pictures Will Talk,* 206n.

19. Koury, *Yes, Mr. DeMille,* 300–302.

5. Mankiewicz and the Making of the Myth

1. SDG Minutes, October 22, 1950, 132. Information concerning the term "black Republicans" from Emeritus Professor John Salmond, personal communication to author, January 24, 2011.

2. Geist, *Pictures Will Talk,* 205; Anthony Miller, "Julius Caesar in the Cold War: The Houseman-Mankiewicz Film," *Literature/Film Quarterly* 28, no. 2 (2000), https://www.questia.com/library/journal/1P3-57006568/julius-caesar-in-the-cold-war-the-houseman-mankiewicz (accessed December 8, 2010). Various accounts have argued that Mankiewicz was involved with the lobby group. See, for

example, Joseph G. Morgan, *The Vietnam Lobby: The American Friends of Vietnam, 1955–1975* (Chapel Hill: University of North Carolina Press, 1997), 34; American Friends of Vietnam papers, Box 14, University Archives and Historical Collections, Michigan State University, East Lansing, quoted in Seth Jacobs, *America's Miracle Man in Vietnam: Ngo Dinh Diem, Religion, Race, and U.S. Intervention in Southeast Asia* (Durham, NC: Duke University Press, 2004), 302; Kevin Lewis, "The Third Force: Graham Greene and Joseph L. Mankiewicz's *The Quiet American*," *Film History* 10, no. 4 (1998): 481.

3. Geist, *Pictures Will Talk,* 346–63; Bosley Crowther, "The Screen: 'Cleopatra' Has Premiere at Rivoli: 4-Hour Epic Is Tribute to Its Artists' Skills," *New York Times,* June 13, 1963; Judith Crist, "Cleopatra: A Monumental Mouse," *New York Herald Tribune,* June 13, 1963; Dauth, *Joseph L. Mankiewicz,* 47; Peter Stone, "All About Joe," *Interview,* August 1989, 181–82; Jeff Laffel, "Joseph L. Mankiewicz," *Films in Review,* July–August and September–October 1991, 198–99.

4. Andrew Sarris, *The American Cinema: Directors and Directions, 1929–1968* (Chicago: University of Chicago Press, 1985), 161.

5. Bogdanovich, *John Ford,* 19.

6. See Youngerman, *My Seventy Years at Paramount Studios,* 91–92; Joseph Mankiewicz interview with Susan Winslow, August 14, 1981, in George Stevens: A Filmmaker's Journey Special Collection, MHL; Geist, *Pictures Will Talk,* 400.

7. Parrish, *Growing Up in Hollywood,* 201–10; Robert Parrish to Joseph Mankiewicz, January 31, 1975, and Joseph Mankiewicz to Robert Parrish, March 21, 1975, Joseph L. Mankiewicz papers, MHL.

8. *Variety,* October 24, 1950, which had the subheading "Marshall is mum." The interview of Robert Parrish with Barry Norman features in the BBC documentary *Ready When You Are, Mr. DeMille* (1981), and it is also presented in Norman, *The Film Greats,* 206–8.

9. Parrish, *Growing Up in Hollywood,* 205; Greg Mitchell, *Tricky Dick and the Pink Lady: Richard Nixon vs. Helen Gahagan Douglas—Sexual Politics and the Red Scare, 1950* (New York: Random House, 1998). The section on the SDG meeting was adapted for an article in the *New York Times,* January 25, 1998. See also J. Hoberman, *An Army of Phantoms: American Movies and the Making of the Cold War* (New York: New Press, 2011), 146. Christopher Bray also made the connection in "Cecil B DeMille: Too Much of the Witchfinder-General," *Daily Telegraph,* December 22, 2007.

10. Joseph Mankiewicz to Tom Guinzburg, "Cecil B. DeMille's Impeachment of Me as President by Joseph L. Mankiewicz," undated, Joseph L. Mankiewicz papers, MHL; Cecil B. DeMille to Tom Girdler, draft letter, May 28, 1954, Box 1163, Folder 6, CBDM; Michael Cieply, "The Night They Dumped DeMille," *Los Angeles Times,* June 4, 1987.

11. Kenneth L. Geist, "Mankiewicz: The Thinking Man's Director," *American*

Film 3, no. 6 (1978): 54–60; Geist, *Pictures Will Talk,* 173–206. Commentators who have argued along similar lines to Geist include Bernard F. Dick, *Joseph L. Mankiewicz* (Boston: Twayne, 1983), 87, 93; Navasky, *Naming Names,* 179–81; Scott Eyman, *Empire of Dreams: The Epic Life of Cecil B. DeMille* (New York: Simon and Schuster, 2010), 411; Lower and Palmer, *Joseph L. Mankiewicz,* 221, 267.

12. *Ready When You Are, Mr. DeMille!* (London: BBC, 1981); the text of this documentary is substantially repeated in Norman, *The Film Greats,* 206–7.

13. Michel Ciment, *Passeport pour Hollywood: Entretiens avec Wilder, Huston, Mankiewicz, Polanski, Forman, Wenders* (Paris: Seuil, 1987), 225–27.

14. Geist interview in Ed Sikov, *On Sunset Boulevard: The Life and Times of Billy Wilder* (New York: Hyperion, 1998), 332; *George Stevens: A Filmmaker's Journey* (dir. George Stevens Jr., 1984); Fred Zinnemann, transcript of filmed interview with George Stevens Jr., November 3, 1982, George Stevens: A Filmmaker's Journey Special Collection, MHL; Vincent Deveau, "Honoring the Artistry of Zinnemann," in *Fred Zinnemann: Interviews,* edited by Gabriel Miller (Jackson: University Press of Mississippi, 2005), 140–41.

15. Joseph Mankiewicz to George Stevens Jr., May 24, 1978; Joseph Mankiewicz interview with George Stevens Jr., November 3, 1982, and Joseph Mankiewicz interview with Susan Winslow, August 14, 1981, George Stevens: A Filmmaker's Journey Special Collection, MHL; David Robb, "Directors Guild Born out of Fear 50 Years Ago," *Variety,* October 29, 1985.

16. Mankiewicz copy of the SDG Minutes, October 22, 1950, facing page 47, 120, Joseph L. Mankiewicz papers, MHL; *Variety,* October 24, 1950; Speech of Cecil B. DeMille to the Screen Directors Guild, Box 1210, Folder 10, CBDM. At points in the speech DeMille did break from the notes, but there is no substantial variation.

17. John Rankin in Congressional Record, vol. 93, part 7, November 24, 1947, 10792, quoted in Gabler, *An Empire of Their Own,* 370–71; Senator Gerald Nye in *Propaganda in Motion Pictures—Hearings before a Subcommittee of the Committee on Interstate Commerce, United States Senate, Seventy-Seventh Congress, First Session on S. Res. 152,* September 9–26, 1941 (Washington, DC: U.S. Government Printing Office, 1942), http://babel.hathitrust.org/cgi/pt?view=text;size=100;id=mdp.39015020646066;page=root;seq=9;orient=0 (accessed February 1, 2009).

18. Parrish, *Growing Up in Hollywood,* 201–10; Catherine Wyler, personal communication to author, May 18, 2010; Eddie Salven's account in Wilcoxon and Orrison, *Lionheart in Hollywood,* 201–2; Axel Madsen, *William Wyler: The Authorized Biography* (New York: Crowell, 1973), 304; Samuel Fuller with Christa Lang Fuller and Jerome Henry Rudes, *A Third Face: My Tale of Writing, Fighting, and Filmmaking* (New York: Knopf, 2002), 273–75.

19. Sikov, *On Sunset Boulevard,* 332. Eyman, *Print the Legend,* 382; Richard Fleischer, *Just Tell Me When to Cry: A Memoir* (New York: Carroll and Graf, 1993),

82; "An Interview with Blacklisted Director Vincent Sherman!," posted by Troma, December 11, 2011, YouTube, https://www.youtube.com/watch?v=eV99RJ9B9Gs (accessed July 15, 2015).

20. Elia Kazan, *A Life* (New York: Anchor, 1989), 391–92. The full transcript of the interview is in the Mankiewicz papers: Interview of Joseph Mankiewicz, September 1984, Joseph L. Mankiewicz papers, MHL. The story about Stevens has appeared in several different versions. It appeared first in the *Daily Worker*—a Communist Party paper—in their report on the October 22 meeting (*Daily Worker*, October 24, 1950), but it is not mentioned in the transcript. Phil Koury quoted it in his 1959 account when he wrote that a director at the SDG meeting on October 22, 1950—presumably George Stevens, who filmed the Battle of the Bulge— said he was "wallowing in the muck of Bastogne at the time that DeMille was defending his capital gains in Hollywood." Koury, *Yes, Mr. DeMille*, 302. Mankiewicz relayed a more ribald version to Parrish, who softened the comment to say: "Another director said he was in Bastogne when DeMille was defending his capital gains in Hollywood." Joseph Mankiewicz to Robert Parrish, March 21, 1975, Joseph L. Mankiewicz papers, MHL; Parrish, *Growing Up in Hollywood*, 208. In another account, Cecil B. DeMille once told Stevens at an SDG board meeting, "I've been fighting this [Communist] problem here in Los Angeles, what have you done?" Stevens replied, "While you were making your capital gains, I was in Bastogne." This was meant to occur in 1947 in debates concerning the statement of Sam Wood to HUAC. This seems to be the most unlikely, as DeMille was not on the SDG board at this time. Eyman, *Print the Legend*, 377. Like many oral statements, it may be a true incident that shows the friction between Stevens and DeMille, but it is not possible to determine when it was said or in what context.

21. *50 Years of Action* (dir. Douglass Stewart), documentary for DGA Golden Jubilee, 1987; Lower and Palmer, *Joseph L. Mankiewicz*, 270. Lower and Palmer date the award as 1991, but this is the same as the list on the DGA website. See also Dauth, *Joseph L. Mankiewicz*, xiv.

22. Michael Cieply, "The Night They Dumped DeMille," *Los Angeles Times*, June 4, 1987.

23. *DGA Moments in Time*, "Part 3: One Night in October," 2011, Directors Guild of America, http://www.dga.org/Craft/75th-Anniversary/75th-Anniversary-Films.aspx (accessed February 4, 2012).

6. Ford's Heroic Stand

1. One of the more recent examples is Joseph Malham, *John Ford: Poet in the Desert* (Chicago: Lake Street Press, 2013), 205.

2. SDG Minutes, October 22, 1950, 21; Douglas Sirk and Jon Halliday, *Sirk on Sirk: Interviews with Jon Halliday* (London: Secker and Warburg for the British Film Institute, 1971), 138.

3. Sarris, *The American Cinema*, 48; Jean-Luc Godard, "Prisoner of the Desert," in McBride, *Searching for John Ford*, 565.

4. Bogdanovich, *John Ford*, 19; Sarris, *The American Cinema*, 43–49; Russell Campbell, "Fort Apache," *Velvet Light Trap: A Critical Journal of Film & Television*, no. 2 (August 1971): 8; Nancy Schwartz, "The Role of Women in Seven Women," *Velvet Light Trap: A Critical Journal of Film & Television*, no. 2 (August 1971): 22. A study by David Mueul, *Women in the Films of John Ford* (Jefferson, NC: McFarland, 2014), challenges the idea that Ford represented women poorly. Another view is from Michael Dempsey, "John Ford: A Reassessment," *Film Quarterly* 28, no. 4, special book issue (Summer 1975): 3–4.

5. *John Ford: The American Film Institute Life Achievement Awards* (World Vision Home Video, 1991).

6. Geist, *Pictures Will Talk*, 203; Ford, *Pappy*, 71–74, 226–27; Andrew Sinclair, *John Ford: A Biography* (New York: Lorrimer, 1984), 157–58.

7. Peter Bogdanovich, "The Cowboy Hero and the American West . . . As Directed by John Ford," *Esquire*, December 1983; reprinted in Kevin L. Stoehr and Michael C. Connolly, *John Ford in Focus: Essays on the Filmmaker's Life and Work* (Jefferson, NC: McFarland, 2008), 7–14.

8. Lindsay Anderson, *About John Ford* (London: Plexus, 1981), 150.

9. Ronald L. Davis, *John Ford: Hollywood's Old Master* (Norman: University of Oklahoma Press, 1995), 245. In the John Ford–John Wayne films, the Wayne character entered a town for personal revenge in *Stagecoach* (1939) and then escaped its corruption. He ambushed a villain in *The Man Who Shot Liberty Valance* (1962). He entered no such fray in *Fort Apache* (1948), *She Wore a Yellow Ribbon* (1949), or *The Searchers* (1956). Perhaps Davis was thinking more along the lines of the Howard Hawks–John Wayne films where Wayne is a law enforcement officer who settles things down in the community. Eyman, *Print the Legend*, 385–87.

10. Garry Wills, *John Wayne's America* (New York: Simon and Schuster, 1997), 162; Brian Spittles, *John Ford* (Harlow, UK: Longman, 2002), 68–70.

11. Joseph McBride, "The Convoluted Politics of John Ford," *Los Angeles Times*, June 3, 2001; McBride, *Searching for John Ford*, 416–17, 473, 483.

12. Edward Buscombe, letter, *London Review of Books*, October 23, 2003. Edward Buscombe's books on Ford include *The Searchers*, BFI Film Classics (London: British Film Institute, 2000). Another correspondent, Andrew O'Hagan, also wrote about Ford's "fudging" on the issues of the blacklist in the same issue. Birchard, *Cecil B. DeMille's Hollywood*, 344.

13. *John Ford/John Wayne: The Filmmaker and the Legend*, American Masters, PBS, broadcast May 10, 2006; Ken Bowser, "Pappy and the Duke," American Masters, May 10, 2006, http://www.pbs.org/wnet/americanmasters/episodes/john-ford-and-john-wayne/pappy-and-the-duke/594/ (accessed July 28, 2010).

14. Johnston's statement came from Murray Schumach, *The Face on the Cutting*

Room Floor: The Story of Movie and Television Censorship (New York: Da Capo, 1975), 129, with no reference. McBride placed the quotes in the right context in *Searching for John Ford,* 464. *Department of State Appropriation Bill for 1948,* 80th Congress, 1st Session, Congressional Testimonies, March 3 (Washington, DC: U.S. Government Printing Office, 1947), 24–25, retrieved from The George C. Marshall Foundation, http://marshallfoundation.org/library/digital-archive/department-state-appropriation-bill-1948/ (accessed November 8, 2014); *Hearings;* W. B. Smith to Eric Johnston, August 7, 1947, COMPIC.

15. Sam B. Girgus, *Hollywood Renaissance: The Cinema of Democracy in the Era of Ford, Capra, and Kazan* (New York: Cambridge University Press, 1998), 19–22, 179.

16. Gaylyn Studlar and Matthew Bernstein, introduction to *John Ford Made Westerns: Filming the Legend in the Sound Era,* edited by Gaylyn Studlar and Matthew Bernstein (Bloomington: Indiana University Press, 2001), 1–2. The same idea of DeMille attacking Mankiewicz's alleged Communism is repeated later in the book, in an essay by Joan Dagle titled "Linear Patterns and Ethnic Encounters in the Ford Western," 103.

17. Jim Kitses, *Horizons West: Directing the Western from John Ford to Clint Eastwood* (London: British Film Institute, 2007), 27, 133n; John Marini, "Defending the West: John Ford and the Creation of the Epic Western," in *Print the Legend: Politics, Culture, and Civic Virtue in the Films of John Ford,* edited by Sidney A. Pearson (Lanham, MD: Lexington Books, 2009), 1–20; Sirk and Halliday, *Sirk on Sirk,* 138.

18. Davis, *John Ford,* 244–45; Sinclair, *John Ford,* 157; Ben Schwartz, "The Subversive St. Patrick's Day Classic: How John Ford Fought McCarthyism with 'The Quiet Man,'" *New Republic,* March 16, 2013, http://www.newrepublic.com/article/112666/john-fords-quiet-man-subversive-st-patricks-day-staple (accessed March 3, 2015).

7. DeMille as Anti-Communist Ogre

1. Sarris, *The American Cinema,* 91.

2. Charles Higham, *Cecil B. DeMille: A Biography of the Most Successful Film Maker of Them All* (New York: Scribner, 1973), 278–79; Joseph Mankiewicz to Robert Parrish, March 21, 1975, Joseph L. Mankiewicz papers, MHL; Parrish, *Growing Up in Hollywood,* 205. Works that repeat the claim include Andrew Sinclair, *John Ford: A Biography* (New York: Lorrimer, 1984), 157; Nora Sayre, *Running Time: The Films of the Cold War* (New York: Dial, 1979), 207; Navasky, *Naming Names,* 179; Brown, *Mabel Walker Willebrandt,* 236; McBride, *Searching for John Ford,* 480; Hoberman, *An Army of Phantoms,* 145n; Nollen, *Three Bad Men,* 218. Norman, *The Film Greats,* 206, repeats the claim but does correctly name the foundation.

3. Center for Legislative Archives, personal communication to author, August 28, 2009.

4. DeMille to Mundt, February 6, 1945, Box 392, Folder 1, CBDM, quoted in Eyman, *Empire of Dreams,* 382; J. Parnell Thomas to Cecil B. DeMille, March 24, 1947, and Cecil B. DeMille to J. Parnell Thomas, March 24, 1947, Box 1154, Folder 10, CBDM.

5. DeMille to Senator Jack B. Tenney, May 3, 1952, Box 1174, Folder 11, CBDM; "List of Political Affiliations of 25 directors in support of Mankiewicz," Box 1210, Folder 10, CBDM; Cecil B. DeMille to Maurice Ries, March 16, 1956, Box 1146, Folder 4, CBDM.

6. Wilcoxon and Orrison, *Lionheart in Hollywood,* 197–98; Cecil B. DeMille to Eugene J. Blum, September 11, 1952, Box 1168, Folder 4, CBDM; Anne Edwards, *The DeMilles: An American Family* (London: Collins, 1988), 219.

7. Koury, *Yes, Mr. DeMille,* 297; Don Whitehead, *The FBI Story: A Report to the People* (New York: Cardinal, 1963), 251.

8. J. Edgar Hoover to SAC Los Angeles, December 13, 1941; Richard Hood to J. Edgar Hoover, December 22, 1941; Richard Hood to J. Edgar Hoover, January 7, 1942; D. M. Ladd to E. A. Tamm, February 7, 1942, Cecil B. DeMille file, FBI.

9. G. C. Callan to Mr Ladd, August 31, 1942; report, October 10, 1945; memo to J. Edgar Hoover, April 15, 1945; Richard Hood to J. Edgar Hoover, "Special Service Contacts," September 17, 1951; Richard Hood to J. Edgar Hoover, "Special Service Contacts," November 25, 1950, Cecil B. DeMille file, FBI.

10. Birchard, *Cecil B. DeMille's Hollywood,* 342; DeMille and Hayne, *The Autobiography of Cecil B. DeMille,* 248; Richard Hood to J. Edgar Hoover, "Special Service Contacts," December 16, 1954, and Richard Hood to J. Edgar Hoover, "Special Service Contacts," September 15, 1950, Cecil B. DeMille file, FBI.

11. Kenneth O'Reilly, *Hoover and the Un-Americans: The FBI, HUAC, and the Red Menace* (Philadelphia: Temple University Press, 1983), 91. Eyman, *Empire of Dreams,* 350–51.

12. Edward G. Robinson and Leonard Spigelgass, *All My Yesterdays: An Autobiography* (New York: Signet, 1975), 299–300. For a comprehensive treatment of Robinson and HUAC, see Ross, *Hollywood Left and Right,* 89–130. Cynthia Miller, "Elmer Bernstein," *Guardian,* October 9, 2002; Wilcoxon and Orrison, *Lionheart in Hollywood,* 199–201; Cecilia deMille Presley, personal communication to author, August 28, 2013.

13. Cecil B. DeMille, "While Rome Burns," address to the Economic Club of Detroit, Michigan, April 19, 1948, Cecil B. DeMille file, FBI.

14. SDG Minutes, October 22, 1950, 111.

15. Birchard, *Cecil B. DeMille's Hollywood,* 344; *American Epic* (prod. Kevin Brownlow and Patrick Stanbury, 2004).

16. Ann Harding, "Kevin Brownlow Interview (Part V)," *Ann Harding's Trea-*

sures, November 15, 2010, http://annhardingstreasures.blogspot.com/2010/11/kevin-brownlow-interview-part-v.html (accessed January 28, 2011). This blog was based on an interview by Christine Leteux with Kevin Brownlow recorded in London during September 2008.

17. Eyman, *Empire of Dreams*, 406–7.

18. Patricia Erens, *The Jew in American Cinema* (Bloomington: Indiana University Press, 1984), 225; Alan Nadel, *Containment Culture: American Narratives, Postmodernism, and the Atomic Age* (Durham, NC: Duke University Press, 1995), 112–15.

19. Andrew Bergman, *We're in the Money: Depression America and Its Films* (New York: Elephant, 1992), 112–14; Peter Roffman and Jim Purdy, *The Hollywood Social Problem Film: Madness, Despair, and Politics from the Depression to the Fifties* (Bloomington: Indiana University Press, 1981), 68.

20. Sumiko Higashi, *Cecil B. DeMille: A Guide to References and Resources* (Boston: G. K. Hall, 1985), 134–36; Girgus, *Hollywood Renaissance*, 111, 132, 179.

21. Brown, *Mabel Walker Willebrandt*, 238; Birchard, *Cecil B. DeMille's Hollywood*, 342; undated clipping, Box 1210, Folder 10, CBDM (the *Los Angeles Times* database does not identify the article); *New York Times*, August 22, 1950.

22. "'The Ten Commandments' Was the 'Titanic' of the Silent Era," DeMille's Lost City, http://www.lostcitydemille.com/titanic.html (accessed May 18, 2007).

23. Gary Alan Fine, *Difficult Reputations: Collective Memories of the Evil, Inept, and Controversial* (Chicago: University of Chicago Press, 2001), 32–35.

Conclusion

1. "50 Years: SAG Remembers the Blacklist: Special Edition of the *National Screen Actor,* January 1998," http://www.cobbles.com/simpp_archive/linkbackups/huac_blacklist.htm (accessed April 2, 2016); "Hollywood Remembers Its Red Scare Victims," CNN, October 28, 1997, http://edition.cnn.com/SHOWBIZ/9710/28/blacklist.remembered/ (accessed April 2, 2016); *Hollywood Reporter,* April 6, 1999.

2. Edward Steers Jr., *Blood on the Moon: The Assassination of Abraham Lincoln* (Kentucky: University Press of Kentucky, 2005), 2.

3. Film versions were even suggested. The first was by Richard Brooks in 1987, and then by Mankiewicz's nephew, Don, who was writing a screenplay in 1999. *Los Angeles Times,* June 4, 1987, and *Variety,* April 6, 1999, quoted in Lower and Palmer, *Joseph L. Mankiewicz,* 235.

4. John Huston interview with George Stevens Jr. and Susan Winslow, March 8, 1983, George Stevens: A Filmmaker's Journey Special Collection, MHL.

5. Fred Zinnemann, filmed interview with George Stevens Jr., November 3, 1982, George Stevens: A Filmmaker's Journey Special Collection, MHL; Daniel L. Schacter, *The Seven Sins of Memory: How the Mind Forgets and Remembers* (Boston: Houghton Mifflin, 2001).

6. Fuller, Fuller, and Rudes, *A Third Face,* 273–75.

7. Interview with Anthony Beevor discussing oral accounts of the D-Day landings, in "D-Day and the Templar on Trial," BBC History Program, History Extra, June 5, 2009, http://www.historyextra.com/podcast/d-day-and-templar-trial (accessed April 27, 2016). See also the related article, "D-Day: The Successes and Failures in Focus," *BBC History Magazine,* June 2009, History Extra, http://www.historyextra.com/feature/second-world-war/d-day-successes-and-failures-focus (accessed April 2, 2016). See also interview with Laurence Rees on the BBC History Program, October 2007, discussing his book *Their Darkest Hour: People Tested to the Extreme in WWII* (London: Ebury, 2007), and the related article, "Terrible Choices People Had to Make during the Second World War," *BBC History Magazine,* October 2007, History Extra, http://www.historyextra.com/feature/second-world-war/terrible-choices-people-had-make-during-second-world-war (accessed April 27, 2016).

Selected Bibliography

Primary Sources

Archives

The Cecil B. DeMille Archives; Film/Music Archives; L. Tom Perry Special Collections, Harold B. Lee Library, Brigham Young University, Provo, Utah (CBDM)

Federal Bureau of Investigation (FBI)

Communist Infiltration—Motion Picture Industry (COMPIC)
DeMille, Cecil B.
Ford, John
Hopper, Hedda
House Un-American Activities Committee (HUAC)
Huston, John
Mankiewicz, Joseph
Willebrandt, Mabel

Margaret Herrick Library, Academy of Motion Picture Arts and Sciences, Beverly Hills, California (MHL)

Richard Brooks papers
John Huston papers
Joseph L. Mankiewicz papers
George Stevens: A Filmmaker's Journey Special Collection
Fred Zinnemann papers

Primary Publications

American Business Consultants. *Red Channels: The Report of Communist Influence in Radio and Television.* New York: Counterattack, 1950.

Bentley, E. *Thirty Years of Treason: Excerpts from Hearings before the House Committee on Un-American Activities, 1938–1968.* New York: Thunder's Mouth/ Nation Books, 2002.

Selected Bibliography

Cogley, J. *Report on Blacklisting*. Vol. 1, *Movies*. New York: Fund for the Republic, 1956.

D'Arc, J. V., and S. Higashi. *The Register of the Cecil B. DeMille Archives: MSS 1400*. Provo, Utah: Harold B. Lee Library, Brigham Young University, 1991.

Schrecker, E. *The Age of McCarthyism: A Brief History with Documents*. New York: Palgrave, 2002.

Secondary Sources

Anderson, L. *About John Ford*. London: Plexus, 1981.

Bergman, A. *We're in the Money: Depression America and Its Films*. New York: Elephant, 1992.

Birchard, R. S. *Cecil B. DeMille's Hollywood*. Lexington: University Press of Kentucky, 2004.

Bogdanovich, P. "The Cowboy Hero and the American West . . . As Directed by John Ford." *Esquire*, December 1983.

———. *John Ford*. London: Studio Vista, 1967.

Brown, D. M. *Mabel Walker Willebrandt: A Study of Power, Loyalty, and Law*. Knoxville: University of Tennessee Press, 1984.

Buscombe, E. *The Searchers*. BFI Film Classics. London: British Film Institute, 2000.

Byman, J. *Showdown at High Noon*. Lanham, MD: Scarecrow, 2004.

Campbell, R. "Fort Apache." *Velvet Light Trap: A Critical Journal of Film & Television*, no. 2 (August 1971): 8–12.

Capra, F. *The Name above the Title: An Autobiography*. New York: Vintage Books, 1985.

Casty, A. *Communism in Hollywood: The Moral Paradoxes of Testimony, Silence, and Betrayal*. Lanham, MD: Scarecrow, 2009.

———. *Robert Rossen: The Films and the Politics of a Blacklisted Idealist*. Jefferson, NC: McFarland, 2013.

Ceplair, L., and S. Englund. *The Inquisition in Hollywood: Politics in the Film Community, 1930–60*. Champaign: University of Illinois Press, 2003.

Ciment, M. *Passeport pour Hollywood: Entretiens avec Wilder, Huston, Mankiewicz, Polanski, Forman, Wenders*. Paris: Seuil, 1987.

Coughlan, R. "15 Authors in Search of a Character Named Joseph L. Mankiewicz." *Life*, March 12, 1951, 158–73.

Critchlow, D. T. *When Hollywood Was Right: How Movie Stars, Studio Moguls, and Big Business Remade American Politics*. New York: Cambridge University Press, 2013.

Daniel, D. K. *Tough as Nails: The Life and Films of Richard Brooks*. Madison: University of Wisconsin Press, 2011.

Dauth, B., ed. *Joseph L. Mankiewicz: Interviews*. Jackson: University Press of Mississippi, 2008.

Davies, P., and B. Neve, eds. *Cinema, Politics and Society in America.* Manchester, UK: Manchester University Press, 1981.

Davis, Ronald L. *John Ford: Hollywood's Old Master.* Norman: University of Oklahoma Press, 1995.

DeBauche, L. M. *Reel Patriotism: The Movies and World War I.* Madison: University of Wisconsin Press, 1997.

DeMille, C. B., and D. Hayne. *The Autobiography of Cecil B. DeMille.* London: W. H. Allen, 1960.

de Mille, W. C. *Hollywood Saga.* New York: E. P. Dutton, 1939.

Dick, B. F. *Joseph L. Mankiewicz.* Boston: Twayne, 1983.

Dmytryk, E. *Odd Man Out: A Memoir of the Hollywood Ten.* Carbondale: Southern Illinois University Press, 1996.

Edwards, A. *The DeMilles: An American Family.* London: Collins, 1988.

Erens, P. *The Jew in American Cinema.* Bloomington: Indiana University Press, 1984.

Eyman, S. *Empire of Dreams: The Epic Life of Cecil B. DeMille.* New York: Simon and Schuster, 2010.

———. *Print the Legend: The Life and Times of John Ford.* New York: Simon and Schuster, 1999.

Fine, G. A. *Difficult Reputations: Collective Memories of the Evil, Inept, and Controversial.* Chicago: University of Chicago Press, 2001.

Fleischer, R. *Just Tell Me When to Cry: A Memoir.* New York: Carroll and Graf, 1993.

Ford, D. *Pappy: The Life of John Ford.* Englewood Cliffs, NJ: Prentice Hall, 1979.

Freedland, M. *Hollywood on Trial: McCarthyism's War against the Movies.* London: Robson Books, 2007.

Friedrich, O. *City of Nets: A Portrait of Hollywood in the 1940's.* London: Headline, 1986.

Fuller, S., with C. L. Fuller and J. H. Rudes. *A Third Face: My Tale of Writing, Fighting, and Filmmaking.* New York: Knopf, 2002.

Gabler, N. *An Empire of Their Own: How the Jews Invented Hollywood.* New York: Anchor, 1989.

Geist, K. L. "Mankiewicz: The Thinking Man's Director." *American Film* 3, no. 6 (1978): 54–60.

———. *Pictures Will Talk: The Life and Films of Joseph L. Mankiewicz.* New York: Scribner, 1978.

Girgus, S. B. *Hollywood Renaissance: The Cinema of Democracy in the Era of Ford, Capra, and Kazan.* New York: Cambridge University Press, 1998.

Gladchuk, J. J. *Hollywood and Anticommunism: HUAC and the Evolution of the Red Menace, 1935–1950.* New York: Routledge, 2009.

Harris, M. *Five Came Back: A Story of Hollywood and the Second World War.* New York: Penguin, 2014.

Higashi, S. *Cecil B. DeMille: A Guide to References and Resources.* Boston: G. K. Hall, 1985.

Higham, C. *Cecil B. DeMille: A Biography of the Most Successful Film Maker of Them All.* New York: Scribner, 1973.

Hoberman, J. *An Army of Phantoms: American Movies and the Making of the Cold War.* New York: New Press, 2011.

Horne, G. *Class Struggle in Hollywood, 1930–1950: Moguls, Mobsters, Stars, Reds, and Trade Unionists.* Austin: University of Texas Press, 2001.

———. *The Final Victim of the Blacklist: John Howard Lawson, Dean of the Hollywood Ten.* Berkeley: University of California Press, 2006.

Humphries, R. *Hollywood Blacklists: A Political and Cultural History.* Edinburgh: Edinburgh University Press, 2010.

Huston, J. *An Open Book.* New York: Knopf, 1980.

Jensen, J. M. *The Price of Vigilance.* Chicago: Rand McNally, 1969.

Kahn, G. *Hollywood on Trial: The Story of the Ten Who Were Indicted.* New York: Boni and Gaer, 1948.

Kazan, E. *A Life.* New York: Anchor, 1989.

Kitses, J. *Horizons West: Directing the Western from John Ford to Clint Eastwood.* London: British Film Institute, 2007.

Koury, P. *Yes, Mr. DeMille: A Humorous and Candid Appraisal of an Extraordinary Showman.* New York: Putnam, 1959.

Levy, B. *John Ford: A Bio-Bibliography.* Westport, CT: Greenwood, 1998.

Louvish, S. *Cecil B. DeMille and the Golden Calf.* London: Faber, 2007.

Lower, C. B., and R. B. Palmer. *Joseph L. Mankiewicz: Critical Essays with an Annotated Bibliography and a Filmography.* Jefferson, NC: McFarland, 2001.

Madsen, A. *William Wyler: The Authorized Biography.* New York: Crowell, 1973.

Malham, J. *John Ford: Poet in the Desert.* Chicago: Lake Street Press, 2013.

Mayer, G. "A Parallel Universe? Hollywood in the 'Pre-code Era.'" *Screening the Past,* March 1, 2000.

McBride, J. "The Convoluted Politics of John Ford." *Los Angeles Times,* June 3, 2001.

———. *Frank Capra: The Catastrophe of Success.* New York: Simon and Schuster, 1992.

———. *Searching for John Ford: A Life.* New York: St. Martin's, 2001.

Miller, G., ed. *William Wyler: Interviews.* Jackson: University Press of Mississippi, 2010.

———, ed. *Fred Zinnemann: Interviews.* Jackson: University Press of Mississippi, 2005.

Mitchell, G. *Tricky Dick and the Pink Lady: Richard Nixon vs. Helen Gahagan Douglas—Sexual Politics and the Red Scare, 1950.* New York: Random House, 1998.

Nadel, A. *Containment Culture: American Narratives, Postmodernism, and the Atomic Age.* Durham, NC: Duke University Press, 1995.

Navasky, V. S. *Naming Names*. London: Penguin, 1991.

Neve, B. *Film and Politics in America: A Social Tradition*. London: Routledge, 1992.

———. *The Many Lives of Cy Endfield: Film Noir, the Blacklist, and* Zulu. Madison: University of Wisconsin Press, 2015.

Nollen, S. A. *Three Bad Men: John Ford, John Wayne, Ward Bond*. London: McFarland, 2013.

Norman, B. *The Film Greats*. Oxford: ISIS, 1985.

Olson, J. S., and R. Roberts. *John Wayne: American*. Lincoln: University of Nebraska Press, 1995.

O'Reilly, K. *Hoover and the Un-Americans: The FBI, HUAC, and the Red Menace*. Philadelphia: Temple University Press, 1983.

Parrish, R. *Growing Up in Hollywood*. London: Bodley Head, 1976.

Pearson, S. A., Jr., ed. *Print the Legend: Politics, Culture, and Civic Virtue in the Films of John Ford*. Lanham, MD: Lexington Books, 2009.

Rich, J. *Warm Up the Snake: A Hollywood Memoir*. Ann Arbor: University of Michigan Press, 2006.

Robinson, E. G., and L. Spigelgass. *All My Yesterdays: An Autobiography*. New York: Signet, 1975.

Rockwell, L. G. "Book Reviews." *American Political Science Review* 47, no. 1 (1953): 211.

Roffman, P., and J. Purdy. *The Hollywood Social Problem Film: Madness, Despair, and Politics from the Depression to the Fifties*. Bloomington: Indiana University Press, 1981.

Ross, S. J. *Hollywood Left and Right: How Movie Stars Shaped American Politics*. New York: Oxford University Press, 2011.

Salmond, J. A. *The Conscience of a Lawyer: Clifford J. Durr and American Civil Liberties, 1899–1975*. Tuscaloosa: University of Alabama Press, 1990.

Sarris, A. *The American Cinema: Directors and Directions, 1929–1968*. Chicago: University of Chicago Press, 1985.

Schacter, D. L. *The Seven Sins of Memory: How the Mind Forgets and Remembers*. Boston: Houghton Mifflin, 2001.

Schumach, M. *The Face on the Cutting Room Floor: The Story of Movie and Television Censorship*. New York: Da Capo, 1975.

Schwartz, B. "The Subversive St. Patrick's Day Classic: How John Ford Fought McCarthyism with 'The Quiet Man.'" *New Republic*, March 16, 2013. http://www.newrepublic.com/article/112666/john-fords-quiet-man-subversive-st-patricks-day-staple.

Schwartz, N. "The Role of Women in Seven Women." *Velvet Light Trap: A Critical Journal of Film & Television*, no. 2 (August 1971): 22.

Schwartz, N. L., and S. Schwartz. *The Hollywood Writers' Wars*. New York: Knopf, 1982.

Sherman, V. *Studio Affairs: My Life as a Film Director.* Lexington: University Press of Kentucky, 1996.

Sikov, E. *On Sunset Boulevard: The Life and Times of Billy Wilder.* New York: Hyperion, 1998.

Sinclair, A. *John Ford: A Biography.* New York: Lorrimer, 1984.

Sirk, D., and J. Halliday. *Sirk on Sirk: Interviews with Jon Halliday.* London: Secker and Warburg for the British Film Institute, 1971.

Spittles, B. *John Ford.* Harlow, UK: Longman, 2002.

Sragow, M. *Victor Fleming: An American Movie Master.* New York: Pantheon Books, 2008.

Steers, E., Jr. *Blood on the Moon: The Assassination of Abraham Lincoln.* Lexington: University Press of Kentucky, 1982.

Stoehr, K. L., and M. C. Connolly. *John Ford in Focus: Essays on the Filmmaker's Life and Work.* Jefferson, NC: McFarland, 2008.

Studlar, G., and M. Bernstein. *John Ford Made Westerns: Filming the Legend in the Sound Era.* Bloomington: Indiana University Press, 2001.

Theoharis, A. G. *The FBI and American Democracy: A Brief Critical History.* Lawrence: University Press of Kansas, 2004.

Ulmer, J. "A Guild Divided." *DGA Quarterly* 2, no. 4 (2006).

Vaughn, R. *Only Victims: A Study of Show Business Blacklisting.* New York: G. P. Putnam, 1972.

Vaughn, S. *Ronald Reagan in Hollywood: Movies and Politics.* Cambridge: Cambridge University Press, 1994.

Whitehead, D. *The FBI Story: A Report to the People.* New York: Cardinal, 1963.

Wilcoxon, H., and K. Orrison. *Lionheart in Hollywood: The Autobiography of Henry Wilcoxon.* Metuchen, NJ: Scarecrow, 1991.

Wills, G. *John Wayne's America.* New York: Simon and Schuster, 1997.

Youngerman, J. C. *My Seventy Years at Paramount Studios and the Directors Guild of America.* Based on interviews by Ira Skutch and David Shepard. Los Angeles: Directors Guild of America, 1995.

Index

Screen Classics

Screen Classics is a series of critical biographies, film histories, and analytical studies focusing on neglected filmmakers and important screen artists and subjects, from the era of silent cinema to the golden age of Hollywood to the international generation of today. Books in the Screen Classics series are intended for scholars and general readers alike. The contributing authors are established figures in their respective fields. This series also serves the purpose of advancing scholarship on film personalities and themes with ties to Kentucky.

Series Editor
Patrick McGilligan

Books in the Series

Mae Murray: The Girl with the Bee-Stung Lips
  Michael G. Ankerich
Hedy Lamarr: The Most Beautiful Woman in Film
  Ruth Barton
Rex Ingram: Visionary Director of the Silent Screen
  Ruth Barton
Conversations with Classic Film Stars: Interviews from Hollywood's Golden Era
  James Bawden and Ron Miller
Von Sternberg
  John Baxter
Hitchcock's Partner in Suspense: The Life of Screenwriter Charles Bennett
  Charles Bennett, edited by John Charles Bennett
My Life in Focus: A Photographer's Journey with Elizabeth Taylor and the Hollywood Jet Set
  Gianni Bozzacchi with Joey Tayler
Hollywood Divided: The 1950 Screen Directors Guild Meeting and the Impact of the Blacklist
  Kevin Brianton
Ziegfeld and His Follies: A Biography of Broadway's Greatest Producer
  Cynthia Brideson and Sara Brideson
The Marxist and the Movies: A Biography of Paul Jarrico
  Larry Ceplair
Dalton Trumbo: Blacklisted Hollywood Radical
  Larry Ceplair and Christopher Trumbo
Warren Oates: A Wild Life
  Susan Compo
Crane: Sex, Celebrity, and My Father's Unsolved Murder
  Robert Crane and Christopher Fryer
Jack Nicholson: The Early Years
  Robert Crane and Christopher Fryer
Being Hal Ashby: Life of a Hollywood Rebel
  Nick Dawson
Bruce Dern: A Memoir
  Bruce Dern with Christopher Fryer and Robert Crane
Intrepid Laughter: Preston Sturges and the Movies
  Andrew Dickos
John Gilbert: The Last of the Silent Film Stars
  Eve Golden

www.ingramcontent.com/pod-product-compliance
Lightning Source LLC
Chambersburg PA
CBHW020455100426
42813CB00031B/3370/J